Network Marketing

Published by:
Lotus Press : Publishers & Distributors

Network Marketing

Arun Mahapatra

Lotus PRESS
4735/22, Prakash Deep Building
Ansari Road, Darya Ganj,
New Delhi-110002

Lotus Press : Publishers & Distributors
Unit No. 220, 2nd Floor, 4735/22, Prakash Deep Building,
Ansari Road, Darya Ganj, New Delhi- 110002
Ph.: 32903912, 23280047 • E-mail : lotus_press@sify.com
www.lotuspress.co.in

Network Marketing

ISBN: 978-81-8382-282-4

Published by : **Lotus Press : Publishers & Distributors** New Delhi-110002
Printed at : Concept Imprint, Delhi

PREFACE

Network Marketing, also known as multi-level marketing (MLM) is a legitimate business model that uses direct selling and relationship referrals as a method of selling a company's products or services. In a typical networking model, individual associates essentially contract or act like a franchisee to the parent company and are paid a commission based on the volume of product or services that are sold as a result of their own organization's efforts.

Just like any other company that sells goods or services the ultimate goal of a network marketing company is to make sales and increase its customer base. Instead of using the traditional method of manufacturing and delivering their products, MLM companies choose to bypass the middleman, selling direct to the customer. They use referrals and a word-of-mouth approach to develop their customer base as opposed to a large advertising budget and as such the money that would normally go to the middleman and advertising can now be used to reward business operators a commission for helping the company to make a sale.

This book provides the best, most authoritative, and up-to-date source of information on the state of network marketing at the turn of the 21st century. It also give readers a wealth of savvy advice on everything one need to know to succeed in network marketing.

—*Arun Mahapatra*

CONTENTS

1

WHAT IS NETWORK MARKETING?

The simplest explanation of network marketing is that it is a method of marketing that utilises independent representatives to reach potential customers that a company otherwise would not reach with traditional online or offline marketing methods. In order to accomplish this, network marketing companies and their associates recruit individuals, i.e., "their sales force," just like other companies and franchises, have done for years, take for example the insurance industry. Network marketing is also popularly known as multi-level marketing (MLM), affiliate marketing, and tiered marketing.

Network marketing is a business model and a legitimate business that uses several methods such as referral programmes and direct selling to sell company products or services. In this business model, individual associates or distributors act like the franchise to the parent company or network marketing business company and they are paid with the compensation according to the number of products sold with their efforts or with their own organization.

Most people confuse network marketing business with the pyramid selling but the fact is that in the network marketing nobody loses money. The profit made by this business model is shared to the individual in this business based on the retail sales and group profits made by them. It is very important for the newcomers in the business to check whether the company is legitimate before signing any contract with them.

While networking marketing is not actually a franchising model of business, it does work in a similar fashion. In fact, some large MLM companies refer to its business plan informally as "private franchising". In network marketing, a company distributes its products and services through independent business owners (IBO) who in turn market these products and services to customers of their own.

The key factor that has made network marketing so attractive is that independent business owners not only have the ability to sell products and services to retail customers they are also able to expand their business by setting up others in their own businesses as well. This is commonly known as "sponsoring" in the MLM industry. Sponsoring others allow a business owner to not only profit from what he directly sells, but also allows him to profit from the sales production of those he has sponsored.

HISTORY OF NETWORK MARKETING

The history of network marketing originates back to the 1940's where a company trading under the name of "California Vitamins" discovered they could make more sales when they had a lot of sales representatives selling a small amount of product each, compared to the traditional business model, of trying to have a few sales representatives selling a lot. California Vitamins also discovered that most of their growing customer base was made up of the friends and family of their existing sales representatives who had essentially referred them to the company as they were impressed with their product line.

New sales representatives were then created from existing satisfied customers and a commission based system was developed. Both teams and individuals were rewarded according to their sales efforts and as a result network marketing was born. The same company later changed their trading name to Nutrilite Food Supplement Corporation.

In 1959, Richard DeVos and Jay Van Andel founded the company Amway which was an abbreviation for the term "the American way". Amway from day one was based on the same network marketing concept. Almost 50 years later Amway is a well established network marketing company operating in more than 80 countries around the world and with more than 3 million business operators.

Currently it is estimated that there are more than 50 million people worldwide involved in network marketing with almost 100 billion in annual wholesale revenue. Given the history of network marketing and it's rapidly growing popularity, the network marketing industry is recognized as one of the fastest growing industries in the world today and is predicted to have significant growth well into the future as more and more companies are choosing to capitalise on this networking trend and choose to sell their products direct to the consumer. This emerging trend is also being driven by a wave of entrepreneurs who continue to drive the concept of improving quality of life and working from home.

Although the history of network marketing dates back to the 1940's it is only now that the industry has come of age. Network marketing has now grown to the point where it is creating more millionaires today than the dot com boom industry did before the bubble burst.

The history of network marketing has stood the test of time and over the past 50 years has proven itself to be a successful distribution model and home-based business opportunity. The industry itself is now currently being endorsed by many business leaders as a proven system for anyone who wishes to achieve financial success. It is not surprising that network marketing is now one of the fastest growing industries of all time with an estimated 150, 000 people just like you, joining the industry every single week.

Given the proven history of the network marketing business model and the emerging business trends the timing could not be better to capitalise on this trend and we encourage all entrepreneurs looking for a home-based business opportunity to seriously consider a network marketing business.

WHY COMPANIES CHOOSE NETWORK MARKETING?

Just like any other company that sells goods or services the ultimate goal of a network marketing company is to make sales and increase its customer base. In a traditional manufacturing company who sell their products to the general public there is normally a large amount of costs associated with advertising and distributing their product (i.e. the middleman is responsible for a lot of the cost), before it is then sold at a retail outlet who again add a profit margin.

Instead of using the traditional method of manufacturing and delivering their products, MLM companies choose to bypass the middleman, selling direct to the customer. They use referrals and a word-of-mouth approach to develop their customer base as opposed to a large advertising budget and as such the money that would normally go to the middleman and advertising can now be used to reward business operators (distributors) a commission for helping the company to make a sale.

There are a number of reasons why many companies are now choosing to use this increasingly popular business model. Firstly, it allows start up companies to build a customer base through referrals without having to try to outspend their competitors advertising budget. Essentially network marketing levels the playing field and allows small businesses the same opportunity as their competing international heavy weights. It also allows the manufacturing company to build a relationship direct with their customers creating better customer satisfaction and loyalty. Selling direct to the customer and bypassing the middleman also helps the customer to save money (without compromising quality), which additionally makes their products more appealing.

Arguably the biggest attraction to joining the industry is that in return for a low risk investment you have the potential to earn a very rewarding residual stream of income whilst enjoying the time freedom to significantly improve your quality of life.

PRINCIPLES OF NETWORK MARKETING

Network marketing success is no accident. It's almost as if there were a bible of success that was written for all of us but very few decided to put into action the principles that were revealed to everyone.

The following are proven principles of network marketing success that are readily available to anyone willing to walk the path:

1. Truly successful network marketers always network. They create massive lists of people matter what type of scenario they may be in. From build up events to generating their own leads using scientific systems or even direct mailing, whatever medium they decide to use you can guarantee the heavy hitters of the MLM industry are constantly

building massive lists of contacts. The purpose of this is that when a unique company launches, they can join this particular opportunity and literally build a massive organization over a matter of weeks.

2. Network marketing success requires that you add value to other people's lives. Successful network marketers are constantly filling their minds up with valuable knowledge to further enhance their MLM business skills and use apply the knowledge to expand their MLM businesses. People love leaders and when they clearly witness the colossal success of true leaders they become attracted to them as someone that can solve their problems and share the 'secrets of success'. Network marketing success is obtained by always adding value. Don't ever stop.
3. Successful network marketers are always taking perpetual action steps. In other words, they reach network marketing success by never giving up. It's a very well known fact that over 90% of network marketers that actually stay in their chosen company for around ten years and are constantly building their business always get to the top the compensation plan. This has happened time and time again and will continue to happen to those that realise this principle.
4. Network marketing success is fueled by the before mentioned. It's the inner drive that is consistently fueling the engine of always forging forward no matter what obstacles arise in their MLM business. The true entrepreneur always seeks solutions to solves issues and problems that do come up up from time to time and are never deterred by this factor. In actuality, they know that having experience and knowledge of how to get around

these pitfalls adds to their value and leadership power whereas most people simply give up and go back to their job.

Network marketing success embodies these principles and they are the foundation of skills and mindset that are necessary if any wealth is to be created in network marketing. Network marketing success demands constant study, network marketing success demands strong will, network marketing success needs devotion, network marketing success requires never giving up and more importantly network marketing success thrives on true leadership.

If you're ready to devote yourself in the proven ways of true network marketing success and have the mindset that it takes to start the journey then it's time to get started. These principles have never failed and never will fail so if the path is taken, then success will come.

NETWORK MARKETING—HOW IT WORK?

Network marketing is an "unseen" business where common people invest small sums of money to create their own business, most commonly through the Internet. Most are created through providing a service or product to the general public. Your first task is to gather customers to buy your product. Next, you must sign up people to partner with you. These people work under you, and you make a profit from their sales and sign-up's, but you will assist them in growing their company, just as someone did for you. The key to making significant money is to have a multitude of people under you.

Time Lines and Commitments

Network marketing, just like a traditional business, is what you make of it. If you are not committed, you will not succeed.

Traditional businesses require thousands of dollars and mountains of time to get off the ground. The usual time frame for success is 3-5 years. Though network marketing requires little to no money down, the time frame for true success remains about the same. The difference is the flexibility with online network marketing. But, if you are not committed to at least 5-20 hours per week, your chances for success drastically decrease. And, your financial obligations are far from over once you've paid the small fee and signed up. What most people neglect to figure in are advertising costs. You would have an advertising budget for a traditional business, so what makes this any different? Nothing! If people don't know what you do or what you sell, they can't be your customers! To honestly succeed, you must network outside the Internet with public presentations or previous professional contacts.

Most MLM's offer training programmes, which is great for you. You get to earn while you learn. But, is it enough? Successful marketing requires a commitment to learning about the business in general, not just your company's philosophy. Seek out marketing training programmes separate from your online company—the more you learn, the more you earn!

Fact or Fiction?

The Internet is jam-packed with multilevel marketing businesses (MLM's), most of which you can start for relatively cheap. Are MLM's just scams on fancy websites? Indeed, some are. This is where your learning comes in—the more you know before you sign up, the more protection you will have against scams. If an offer sounds too good to be true, chances are, it is!

You must first make sure your company is providing a service or product of real value. Many companies pay your dividends from sign-up monies—this is not what you are looking for. Beware of false representation—do your homework! If the company does not provide a unique product or service that the average person uses almost daily—rethink!

Beware of the "multiplier effect". Most companies give you a set number of people to signup under you before you can start making the big bucks. What they fail to clarify is that those signups must be active. Consider this—usually 1 out of every 5 signups will be active. And once they find out the "big bucks" is only a few hundred dollars a month instead of a few thousand, the likelihood that they will drop their status goes way up! This is where your patience and consistency pays-off.

Don't expect exorbitantly high paychecks from the start. Making real money takes time. Expect to beef up monthly income by only a few hundred dollars at first. This may not be enough to quit your job, but with the flexibility network marketing offers, there's nothing wrong with supplementing your present income until considerate monies start rolling in from residual income and steady sales.

How To Get Started?

Getting started in a network marketing business is easy. Usually you express some interest on a website and before you know it, someone is calling you to sign up. The initial expenditures are minimal, so why not, right? Wrong! Before signing up with any company do your homework!

Ask questions. Make sure sponsors are experienced. You need the right mentor to guide you through the startup process and for continued support while you grow your business. Make sure you know what is included. Proper marketing training is essential, and most offer this service. Research the products or services provided. Most companies offer your own website where customers can shop at your own online store, but don't be fooled by flashy websites.

A word of caution for the "free" signup companies—they are less likely to provide you with in-depth training, and unless you are already a successful marketing professional, chances are you will not know enough to make a go of your new venture.

Failure Facts

There are several reasons why you or your company in general fails. The primary reason is lack of education. MLM's are real businesses are require know-how and patience. You wouldn't start a traditional business without proper education—network marketing is no different. Consider these opportunities only if you are serious and committed. Go beyond initial training and never think you know it all!

Beware of false representation. By doing preliminary research before signing on, you decrease your chances of getting into a less-than-reputable company. Make sure the company has experienced managers to assist you throughout. Be wary of ineffective products—make sure they are unique, yet able to be used by the average person. Inquire about recruitment and capital—many MLM's fail due to lack of both.

Another common problem why network marketing fails is lack of commitment. If you, or your company does not take the business serious, you will not succeed. Most network marketing companies are almost too easy to join, leading to rash decisions on your part secondary to bold claims of making millions in a short period of time. MLM's are not a "get-rich-quick" scheme. They require patience and know-how.

Network marketing businesses can be worth the time and effort for the right person. But, as with any new business, it is what you make of it. Sure, they offer you increased flexibility and the option of working at home, but that is no reason to slack off. With a little bit of dedication and know-how, you can turn a small amount of money into success.

NETWORKING, VALUE ADD AND COMMUNICATION

If you are thinking about going into the network marketing industry, be forewarned that only the strongest, the most dedicated, and most diligent people will achieve star quality greatness in network marketing. The only guarantee a network marketing opportunity can offer is that success is dependent not only in your product or service, but also on you and your ability to satisfy your customers' wants and needs.

Know What People Want

Whether you are approaching a person as a business partner or as a customer for your network marketing business, always remember that there are three things that people want.

1. People want to feel that you respect them for the person they are.
2. People want to feel that you care about them and that you are not just interested in recruiting them or selling them something.
3. People want to establish a connection with someone whom they feel they can trust and that can lead them to success in network marketing!

Importance of Networking

Networking is critical in any business; however, in the network marketing industry networking is a long-term investment. While not all of your contacts will be interested in becoming a business partner, many of them are potential customers. To reach them, you must be willing to establish contact and illustrate why your product (s) meets their needs. That store clerk you rudely blew off yesterday may become the huge business builder your network marketing competition recruited and the one that you will forever feel "got away." Treat every person you meet as if your financial future depends on them, because it very well may. When businesses sell you a product, there are often "value add" points that they are using to promote with—a free product, a free service, and superior quality are all value add points.

Discounts, informational newsletters, and coupons are also considered value add points. Agreeing to place a person in a new distributor's downline the moment they enroll would be a huge value add when recruiting. In network marketing, build your business the right way by identifying the things that add value to what you are offering.

If you do it well and do it often, many of your contacts can develop into new customers or partners for your network marketing business. However, remember that no matter how charming, enthusiastic or persuasive you are networking relationships have a short life cycle. Therefore, once you have identified and built your network of business colleagues, family, friends, professional acquaintances, etc., immediately begin turning those contacts into business partners or customers.

Even after building a strong network, this is something you must continually do, as you will lose a certain number of them through reasons you cannot control; they stop using your product because it no longer fits their needs, they can no longer afford it, they become dissatisfied, or even die.

Communication

Equally important is communication. Keep in mind that "communication is like a contact sport, so do it early and often." One of the biggest mistakes people make in network marketing is that they fail to realise the importance of prompt follow-up after introducing someone to the product or company at networking events. If you do not follow up you will likely lose them to someone who is willing to follow through. Send a "thank you" e-mail and see if they have questions that were unanswered at the networking event. Send them the latest copy of your networking newsletter. These steps will ensure that you have reinforced your relationship and your connection with your contact. This is the perfect time to send them information about the network marketing industry that reinforces the business opportunity that you have presented to them.

Even in network marketing, it is rare to meet people at the exact moment in time when they are seeking a business opportunity in the direct sales industry or when they are disillusioned with a product your competitor offers. So when they are ready to pursue a network marketing opportunity or replace a current product they are dissatisfied with, can you be certain that they will remember the opportunity, product, or service that you offered? They will not if you do not make an indelible impression that is long lasting. It is far easier to nurture an existing contact than it is to revive it once it falls by the wayside. It takes time to develop relationships and in network marketing, you must educate the consumer about the industry as well as the product. During the process, you will find you develop many strong, new relationships.

Since the average, repeat customer spends 67% more than new customers, it makes good sense to foster relationships that are providing the most profit for your network marketing business. Stay in touch with customers and potential business partners. Offer them something of value that keeps them connected to you beyond that initial encounter. Identify your "value add" points and then use them effectively.

Teach Others to be Successful

Once your network marketing business is off and running, you may be tempted to sit back, relax, and let someone else do the work for a change. You must continually help and promote your downline of distributors to grow and be successful. You know that teaching and leading by example were key elements that helped you to quickly recruit your first distributor, earn bonuses and residuals, and build a large network marketing organization.

Just like you found out from your enroller/sponsor what it took to be successful and then emulated it, as an enroller/sponsor you too must teach and support those you bring into the business. Sharing your network marketing success story, helping those in your downline to learn the basics, and helping them to develop, execute and follow through on their business plan will foster a relationship that will move each of you closer to your milestones.

If you truly have the desire to be successful in the network marketing industry, jump in with both feet and do not look back. If you stay connected, stay focused, and help your distributors grow their business, they will be forever thankful and you will soon begin to reap the benefits from their commitment to you. Remember network marketing is not just about the money, but also about the relationships and personal growth that you and your team of distributors will experience by coming together and working together.

BECOMING SUCCESSFUL IN NETWORK MARKETING

When you utter the words network marketing, it is possible to illicit a wide array of responses. From the successful marketing guru, to the person who has been "burned" too many times, you will find many different experiences when questioning someone about their network marketing experience. Why is this? Well the simple truth is network marketing is simply not for everyone. While this may seem like a cliché, it is the truth. When involving yourself with network marketing, you have to be self motivated, consistent, patient and knowledgeable about what network marketing really is. However, most people who start their own network marketing business are not willing take on any of the characteristics that make for a successful

To be successful in network marketing, you have to understand that it is a business. You only get out what you put into it. When you have a job, you can go to work and do just what you need to do to get by and yet you will still get paid. This is not the case with network marketing. You have treat network marketing like it is your business. While you may be scared and intimidated to talk to your friends, family members or strangers about the particular product or service you are marketing, you have to remember that you are just introducing them to what it is that you do. Don't tell yourself that you have to be a sales person. You are just introducing your business to them. Remember that some will, some won't, so what...Next. If you remember that you are just sharing information and not selling a product, you will feel more comfortable with telling your family members what it is that you do. Wouldn't you be offended if your sister or brother opened up a gas station and didn't tell you about it? Well you have to think of your network marketing business the same way. The only difference between your sister's gas station and your network marketing business is that in most cases you won't have a brick and mortar type establishment. You will most likely be doing business out of your home or while you are out and about. Again don't try to sell anything. If you choose the right network marketing company, the products or services will sell themselves.

The main reason why people fail at network marketing is because they are not self motivators. Most people are not used to being in the drivers seat of their own financial vehicle because they have bosses who tell them what to do, how to do it and when to do it. When you start a network marketing business, you are in complete control. Sure, you may have the person who introduced you to the opportunity there with you, but ultimately, they can't make you do anything in your network marketing business.

Another major factor that may cause someone to fail in network marketing is lack of consistency. There are plenty of people who at the start of their business may hit the ground running. They may do all that they need to do their first day or week in their business but then when results are not what they expected or when something else comes up, they slow down. In most cases, the reason why people are not consistent is because they get frustrated when people tell them they are not interested in becoming a business owner with them, or that they are not interested in buying a product or service. Let's think about this for a moment. You have to remember what was mentioned earlier and that is you have to share what it is that you do. Take the pressure off of yourself and don't feel as though you have failed because you didn't make a sale. You have done your job as long as you have shared the information with your prospect. Don't let a simple little "no" stop you from being consistent especially if you have only been working for a few days. What if a new restaurant opened up in your town, and on their grand opening day, they only had a few customers. Do you think that they would close down their restaurant? The answer is no.

When you start a network marketing business, don't expect to become wealthy overnight. Also, don't expect it to be easy. Just think about those others who have started their own businesses. Do you think Sam Walton instantly became a millionaire when he opened his first Wal-mart? No he did not, so why should you expect the same thing? The biggest misconception that people have is that they will become wealthy very quickly. While it is possible to make some good money in the beginning stages of your business, you won't become financially free in a few days, weeks, months and in some cases it can take quite a few years. The thing is you have to have patience. If you commit to one year of solid hard work, you will definitely see results. Most people can replace their income and begin focusing solely on their business when they have dedicated a solid year to their business.

There are many other roadblocks that may come up when you are starting a network marketing business, but these are just the basic qualities that one must possess in order to become successful.

The majority of people around the world cannot afford to start a traditional business because start-up costs can be extreme. Network marketing offers people a chance to own their own business with minimal start-up costs. Distributors can then sell products and build and manage their own sales force by recruiting, motivating, supplying, and training others to duplicate their efforts. The distributors' compensation includes their own sales and a percentage of the sales of their sales group (downline). In most cases, distributors are not required to purchase huge amounts of inventory, nor are they required to pay huge entry fees. For a minimal investment, a committed person can become a distributor and build a successful business. Another perk is that network marketing enables distributors to grow and progress at their own pace, achieving success as defined by each individual.

The power of network marketing lies in:

1. Word of mouth advertising (considered the most effective form of advertising today).
2. Sales and distribution channel that bypasses the middle man.
3. Reasonably priced products and services that people consume in a short time.
4. Ability to realise financial gain for helping others build a business.
5. Building an organization of other independent distributors and customers below you (downline), and earning a percentage of their combined sales and/or purchases (Residual Income).
6. Achieving your personal financial goals.

Many people join network marketing companies and are quickly disillusioned when they fail—often not even recouping the cost of their distributor packages. The simplest and most frequent reaction to this failure is to blame the company. However, the fact is that the biggest reason people fail is because they did not understand the industry and had no business plan in place. Simply stated, "If you fail to plan, you plan to fail."

From the moment you say yes to becoming an independent distributor, to the moment you hand over your credit card or write out your check for your new starter kit, you should already be formulating a plan that will immediately propel you in the direction that allows you to soar and expand your new business. This means you must have a dedicated schedule and method for building your business. Always be aware of the fact that your success will be in direct proportion to your personal efforts. It will require hard work and you will encounter skepticism and rejection more often than not. So if you are sensitive to rejection, you may want to shy away from this industry. However, if you realise that network marketing is a numbers game (the law of averages say for every X number of people you approach, a certain percentage will sign up), and keep plugging along, you definitely can succeed.

PROBLEM IN NETWORK MARKETING

Network marketing is just a business model, and it really amounts to "micro-franchising". Its upside is that it has a very low cost of entry, with the potential for exceptional revenue, and there are those who achieve that.

But those same things that make it attractive make it attractive to many who are not really qualified or prepared to become business owners. The salient characteristics of MLM make it attractive to people who:

— have not done well in their business or profession and have little money saved up to invest;

— have no previous experience owning or running a business;

— have no previous experience in sales;

— have little or no experience developing business relationships other than that of employer/employee/co-worker;

— are not satisfied with their current level of income;

— have unrealistic expectations of the amount of work involved compared to the revenue realized.

I'm not saying that there's anything wrong with any of these things, or that this describes even a majority of network marketers—only that it describes a disproportionate number of network marketers, and that many of them never do anything about it.

As a result, many network marketers end up:

- over-selling the opportunity
- inappropriately discussing business in social situations
- coming across as desperate
- over-focused on new recruits and neglecting existing customers as a result
- being either inaccurate or deceptive when talking about their business

Again, I'm certainly not saying that this describes a majority of network marketers, but it does describe enough of them to tarnish the reputation of the rest. To pre-judge someone based on the basis of a small minority of people in that group is horribly unfair, but we must realise that most prejudices have some basis in reality, even if it has been distorted.

There's a first time for everything. And network marketing/MLM is a great opportunity for people to have their first business, their first sales role, etc. Recognise it for what it is: it's a business, and you are a business owner. And if you've never owned a business before, if you've never done sales before, if you've never networked before, you need to learn about how to do so, not just from the network marketing/MLM experts, but from established experts in those fields.

Network marketers who are serious about building a business should be reading and learning about business fundamentals, the latest sales and marketing techniques, strategies for networking and business development, etc., not just swapping tips at your team's weekly or monthly meeting. Act like a small business owner, and people will treat you like one.

❖❖❖

2

ROLE OF VISION IN NETWORK MARKETING

The *Bible* says that without a vision the people perish. What does this mean. It means we need to see where we're going, ahead of time, in order to get there. When someone has a vision, it becomes real when written down or verbalised.

Vision is being able to see, that which will be, even when it is not. Sometimes all our present circumstances, are the evidence that screams out, to resist, our moving towards, our dream of the future.

In network marketing, belief plays a big role, as it does, in life itself. A vision helps us to build belief. When we believe something is going to happen, we'll work towards it. It's like the farmers. They buy seed, till their fields, plant the seeds and wait for the rains. The rains come, the seeds sprout and eventually there's a harvest.

Without a vision of that harvest, and a faith to plant, there would be no harvest.

It's the same for all of us in life. When we first join, a network marketing company, we don't know a whole lot. We know very little about the products, aren't sure how to sell them, or even if we can. We don't have any idea how the compensation plan works, or even, exactly how it all fits together.

What, we do know, is we saw a vision. Somehow in that dvd, cd webinar, internet video, or live presentation, a spark was lite. We saw a new hope for the future. A new belief, in a better way of life, was sparked. In short, we received the vision. It was the same one, all who went before us, had received. For success in network marketing to occur, we must get that same vision.

ATTRACTIONS OF NETWORK MARKETING

Most people who become involved in network marketing are initially attracted for very specific and personal reasons. Of course, one of the most common reasons involves money—and all of the wonderful things that money provides. For others, motivation may come from a desire to pursue a rewarding, fulfilling, and fun occupation. Others may be attracted to the time and personal freedom that this business can offer. Others still may want to become associated with a supportive team who contribute to the lives of others with either extraordinary products or a potentially life-changing income opportunity. Let's examine several of the different areas of motivation first as they apply to you and then as they relate to creating rich value for your prospects.

Perhaps you were initially attracted to network marketing because you saw it as a way to generate a supplemental income stream. Maybe you had a desire to make life a bit easier for yourself and your family by earning an extra few hundred or a few thousand dollars more each month. Maybe you were attracted to the possibility that this business offered a vehicle to earn at least enough for a new car or home payment. Possibly, your intention was to replace your full-time earned income with a residual income that would free you up to pursue other interests and passions.

No matter what your motivation, it will support you to clarify exactly what you hope to attain from your network marketing efforts. Doing so will both allow you to determine the amount of monthly income that would make your efforts in this business worthwhile and serve as the motivation for doing what oftentimes may be inconvenient or uncomfortable. Your ability to gain clarity regarding what motivates you will be the first step in formulating a detailed plan to achieve the level of income that will make the attainment of your goals and dreams possible. For example, if your goal is to earn a royalty income of Rs four lakhs per month within a few years' time, your action plan will need to be considerably more rigorous than if your goal is to cover a monthly car payment.

Oftentimes, those first introduced to network marketing may know that they want to earn a specific amount of money but will not have sufficient clarity regarding for what purpose they will use the money. It is important not only to know how much income you intend to generate but also why you want the income. Money alone is usually not a sufficient motivator to encourage the sort of consistent and persistent daily action required to build a network marketing dynasty. If you are not clear about why you are doing this business, consider the following possibilities as if money were no object:

- Would you continue to work at your present occupation? Would you retire early or cut back on your work schedule?
- Would you continue to live in your current home and neighbourhood? If you'd buy a new house, what would it be like and where would it be located?

- Would you drive a different car and have any new toys?
- How would your family make use of a sizeable recurring income?
- Would you put your children or grandchildren through school?
- Would you pay off all debt and revel in the freedom of being debt-free?
- Would you invest in real estate, stocks, or other investments?
- Would you travel and explore? If so, where?
- Would you go on an extended shopping spree? For what items?
- Would you donate your money or time to a special project or charity?
- Would you pursue any passions or hobbies? Would you take lessons in a craft or sport or develop a new skill?
- Would you develop a secure retirement fund?
- Would you return to school to finish your education or pursue an interest?
- Would you use your network marketing business and the opportunities it provides to take on a personal development programme?
- Would you step into leadership in your company, church, or community?
- Would you partner with friends and family to create a fun and rewarding lifestyle?
- Would you free up your time to coach youth sports or do volunteer work?
- Would you use your free time to undertake programmes to increase your self-esteem and personal confidence level?

In planning how you will impact your world with your network marketing opportunity, you are limited only by your imagination and creativity. As strange as it may seem, some fear the creation of wealth, thinking it will lead to temptation and corruption. How often have you heard it expressed that money is the root of all evil? Money, in and of itself, is neither good nor evil. It is how we decide to utilise our wealth that determines its character. If you may have feared creating wealth for a similar reason, just ponder how much good you could do to ease some of the world's suffering or how you might provide opportunity for those in need with the wealth you could create using network marketing as your vehicle.

Take a few minutes now and identify what you will be achieving with regard to income and identify your reasons for becoming involved in network marketing. Do not allow yourself to be hindered by self-doubt, a lack of belief or clarity in how you will achieve your desired level of income?

CREATE A VISION

Now that you have identified your top reasons for building a business, it's time to transform these motives into a vibrant, passionate vision that will inspire you and those with whom you'll share your vision. Perhaps your motivation to build a business may start out small. Maybe your reasons are conservative in nature. You may be fairly content with your current work and lifestyle. If this describes your situation, your vision will likely look a lot like an extension of your current lifestyle with some specific improvements in certain areas in which your life is not working optimally. However, if you are among the more ambitious who are seeking to build a network marketing dynasty because of a desire to dramatically impact your life and what's possible by living large, your vision will bear little resemblance to a life marked by the typical daily grind that most others are wrapped up in, with all the suffering, struggle, or lack that limits what most believe is possible to attain. For this vision, I'll assume that your motivation stems from a desire to have it all—a thriving network marketing business that supports your dream lifestyle.

Pretend for a moment that a genie has appeared before you. This genie possesses a magic wand that you can wave over your life, allowing you to transform your current existence into a life of choice. The power of this magic wand can touch every aspect of your life. It can create wealth and abundance in your world for you and for those you love. This abundance will allow you to live in choice, no longer needing to suffer because of a lack of material needs. Your decisions about what you'll have in terms of cars, homes, and other material possessions need no longer be limited because of money.

Moreover, this magic will impact your life well beyond money and material goods. It will influence what you do. Your days will be characterised by a newfound freedom that will allow you to do what you want, when you want to do it. Your typical day at work will take on a whole new empowered energy. You'll be living and working in choice—not because you have to do so. You'll no longer have to answer to the demands of a demeaning boss or deal with difficult employees, peers, or subordinates. Nor will you need to fight rush hour traffic or punch that time clock that used to track the pennies you earned, making someone else wealthy. The stresses of working for someone else will evaporate into the contentment that comes from knowing that your efforts are being truly rewarded. You'll now have the vehicle to earn what you're really worth.

Think for a moment about how you will spend your dramatically increased amount of free time. What will a typical day at play look like for you? You'll be able to do all those things you didn't have the time or money to do before. Will that be a favourite sport or hobby? Maybe it will mean more fun time with family and friends. Remember, the genie has put no limitations on what you can do, so why would you continue to do anything that doesn't honour your values or provide you with fulfilment and happiness?

Think about the legacy you can leave on this planet if you have the time and income to contribute to others. How would you contribute and to whom? Would your generosity extend beyond family to friends in need? Would you adopt a philanthropic mission? What would give you such fulfilment that you could spend the next 100 years contributing to this cause? All this will become part of your vision.

Finally, in addition to all the money, material possessions, and time freedom to do all those great things you've always wanted to pursue, you'll now have the luxury to work *on* yourself. With the need to chase a daily earned income in your past, thanks to the consistent flow of residual income coming into your mailbox each month, you can now focus on the challenge of personal development, if you so desire. You can create a plan to expand who you are, develop those qualities you wish others to know you by, and break-through any limitations that have come in the way of achieving happiness and personal fulfilment. Will you be known for your charisma and contribution? Will you be known for authenticity and compassion? Perhaps your life will be all about fun, adventure, and the courage to live passionately and without limitations. For what qualities would you like your children and others you respect to know you? These traits will all be part of the reinvented person and lifestyle you'll clarify in your vision.

VALUES

A vision that inspires you to breakthrough accomplishment must honour your most important values. These values make up the core of who we are.

Some most important human values are:

Love
Fun
Happiness
Compassion
Contribution
Adventure
Beauty
Freedom
Creativity
Peace
Belonging
Communication
Security
Recognition
Family
Humour
Acceptance
Appreciation
Order
Spirituality
Harmony
Safety
Joy
Intimacy

They demand to be honoured. If they are violated, you'll likely become angry, withdrawn, and noncommunicative. As you craft your vision, make sure you design all areas of your life in choice. There need not be any shoulds that result in pain, struggle, and resentment. As the master architect of your future, you can make everything a reflection of your commitment to live responsibly. Taking responsibility for what manifests itself around you means ensuring all aspects of your life work optimally including the quality of your relationships, your health and physical condition, your wealth and financial security, your happiness, the pursuit of your recreations, hobbies, and passions, and your personal and spiritual development. Who says you can't have it all? It's about time you decided to stop settling for less than you deserve!

VISIONS AND SELF-MOTIVATION

Before you take some time to put your own idealised vision down on paper, let's look a bit deeper at some of the reasons for creating a detailed written vision. Ever cry or scream when watching a movie? We know it's just a movie with actors pretending to step into the roles of their characters. But we cry or become afraid anyway. Now close your eyes. Picture someone running his long pointy fingernails down a black chalkboard. Does this visualisation cause a shiver to run down your spine? Perhaps you felt the tingles just by envisioning the scene. The reason for these seemingly illogical responses is that the mind cannot tell the difference between events that are real and those that are vividly imagined. If we can create a vivid mental picture of how our reality will look, sound, smell, and feel, our mind will support us in experiencing it as though it *were* actually real.

Once we create the vivid mental picture of the life we desire, we can then deliberately reinforce these images into our consciousness by daily repetition. By reading our ideal vision daily (once upon rising and once at bedtime is best), it eventually becomes part of our consciousness. The more familiar it becomes, the greater will be our belief in its ultimate realization. Before long, what was once a foreign and difficult concept to grasp will soon become an expectation of what our future will resemble. When such a future appears to be inevitable, we will find ourselves acting in ways that are consistent with its actually happening. The more we can condition our mind to expect such an outcome, the more motivation we will generate to fuel its fulfilment. Do not be limited by thoughts that the vision of your ideal world may be unrealistic and beyond your grasp. The more familiar you become with the concepts presented in your vision statement, the more self-motivated you will become to take the actions necessary to attain your ideals.

The opposite effect holds true as well. If we worry or envision a future that is worse than our current reality, this expectation will result in the creation of self-sabotage. Our mind says, "Okay, we're going to fail anyway, so why should we work so hard and do these inconvenient and uncomfortable actions (like prospect friends, family, and strangers) when our efforts are likely to be futile?"

We justify behaviours that are inconsistent with success and then get to be right about our expectation of failing after all! Self-sabotage can take many forms. Perhaps it will show up as inconsistency in our prospecting actions, working only when we feel like it. Maybe we will fail to follow up with our prospects because we tell ourselves that they are probably not interested anyway. With an expectation of failure, our conversations will also likely lack the enthusiasm, belief, and value critical in the art of enrollment. We expect to fail and fail we do! Then we make excuses for this outcome, often blaming network marketing itself, our company, our upline support team, or any other convenient victim for our own missing belief and lack of action.

Once things start picking up, we'll return to ineffective behaviours consistent with our expectation of more of the same. We'll experience small, incremental changes that are in line with our expectations and actions. The more we experience the same results we have come to expect, the more complacent and apathetic we will become. After all, if things are always likely to stay the same, more or less, why work so hard or become motivated to break through any challenges that may arise? It's no use anyway. We might as well stay safe and secure in the rut we've dug called our comfort zone!

Take a moment now to ask yourself honestly if your current vision for your future is bright and optimistic, negative and depressing, or consistent with what you are currently experiencing. No matter where you now find yourself, you have the ability to craft an empowering and inspirational vision. If we do not deliberately take responsibility for what our lives will be like in every respect, then, by default, we forfeit our ability to choose and create this reality purposefully. If we forgo this right, we must then accept whatever vision others have for our lives. We then lose control over our destiny. Our expectation of having less than we really desire becomes a self-fulfilling prophecy. Like most of the rest of the world's population, we then resign ourselves to a life that neither honours our most important values nor inspires us to be our very best.

It's now time to break this vicious cycle. Your future need not bear a close resemblance to your past. Remember, we *already* have a vision for our futures. For most of us, this is usually just a different version of our past experiences with small, predictable improvements. Just look around you. Do you like what you see? If not, it's now within your power to craft a new and exciting reality to step into. Remember, too, that we will be taking responsibility for manifesting whatever vision we choose to manufacture by designing a detailed plan that will answer the question, "What will it take to manifest this vision deliberately in all respects?"

Your vision will inspire you and fuel your motivation to do whatever it takes to result in its being manifested. By sharing it with others, it will also inspire them to join you in its fulfilment, while creating visions of their own. You will be able to tell the quality and strength of your vision by taking a look at the actions it inspires. As you become adept in crafting your own vivid and compelling vision, you will also be developing the skills necessary to teach others how to create their own empowering visions. Constructing such a vision will always be the first step in building a solid foundation upon which to design the action plan and personal effectiveness structures that will result in the network marketing dynasty you desire.

Not only will your vision fuel your belief level and be the foundation for your action plan, but you will be able to return yourself to your vision whenever the going gets rough and challenges arise, as they are sure to do. Similarly, if your distributors become discouraged and resigned that "this will never work," reminding them of the reasons they became involved in the first place will support them to muster the courage and perseverance needed to hang in there and work toward the realization of their dreams, rather than to quit and forever give up on them.

IMPORT YOUR VISION TO PAPER

It's now time to set aside an hour or two and actually put your vision into words. Your written vision will be most powerful when crafted as an already accomplished scene from a movie depicting your life at some point in time. Write your vision in the first person, present tense. "I am now... I now have... I am doing... I am contributing to..." and so on. Avoid writing in terms of negative behaviour. Instead of writing "I will no longer be poor and overweight," say "I am abundant and healthy." Your mind will key in upon the images created, so craft these images to your advantage. Include in your vision as many sensual references as possible. What are you feeling emotionally? What sights, smells, and sounds are present in the scene you are depicting? What are others who play an important role in your vision saying, doing, and feeling? Make your vision as emotional as possible by focusing upon those areas that will bring you the most joy and fulfilment.

Remember to include as many others in your vision as possible, since a vision that is only about you will not inspire or motivate others in the way one that touches their lives will. You'll know that you've hit the mark when you are inspired by reading what you've written.

❖❖❖

3

PLANNING FOR NETWORK MARKETING

Before you do anything with an online business you need to make sure you have a network marketing business plan and marketing strategy in place. Creating a plan is the most important things that will determine your success or failure.

Mindset and personal development have a lot to do with achieving success, however, you can think positive all day and cite affirmations 'til the cows come home, but without some kind of plan to reach your goals, then all of your affirmations amount to nothing. After you have decided what it is that you want to do with your business, then you need to a marketing plan. Now, don't get this confused with a marketing strategy.

WHAT IS A NETWORK MARKETING BUSINESS PLAN?

Your network marketing business plan is a schedule of what you plan to do everyday in your business. Think of it much like an exercise plan where you setup planned workouts at the beginning of the week for each day. Monday – Back and Biceps, Tuesday – Triceps, Shoulders and Chest, Wednesday – Legs & Back, etc. Setting up this plan will help keep you accountable and focused on your goals. Now, if accountability to yourself isn't enough to keep you on track, find a partner to help you.

You want to set this plan up with realistic times depending upon the amount of time you have. Some of you are still at full-time jobs. So, make sure to space things out and understand you are not going to get everything done in a day, week and maybe not even a month. As an entrepreneur, sometimes there are distractions and technological breakdowns that will delay us. Don't sweat it. Learn to adapt and get right back in there.

Your marketing business plan is what you plan to do, however your marketing strategy is how you plan to do it. It's how you execute the plan. Many get confused on the differences when it comes to developing their marketing plan. It's critical that you understand the differences to keep you on the right path.

Having a solid strategy will help you greatly in your network marketing business but also realise that it is not set in stone. You can always and you should tweak it as you go along. There is no such thing as the perfect plan.

Sometime you may find a new useful site or a new tool that was just released that can help you. This is why your marketing strategy can change as you move forward. You do need to have something solid to start of with though. So having your strategy and marketing plan both solid from the beginning will give you great advantage over your competition. Trust me on that!

You all remember the story about the two men who built their homes – one built on sand and the other built on rock. Sure, the guy who built on sand was quicker and finished his house faster than the guy who built on rock.

He would point and laugh at the other guy while sipping lemonade on his porch, straight chillin'. "Look at this fool using rock to build his home. It'll take him forever to get that house done."

BUSINESS PLAN: CORE BEHAVIOURS

Now that you have a vision in place that inspires accomplishment, let's look at what actions are necessary to manifest this vision in the world. Of course, the very heart of any business plan will involve three core behaviours:

1. Use your company's products or services. Always choose your own company's products over those offered by all competitors, and buy from your own business. Become familiar with all your products' applications and the differentiating qualities that make them so special and desirable. Develop an unshakable belief in the value of the income opportunity that your products make possible.
2. Recommend your products or services to others everywhere and on a daily basis. Establish an ever-growing list of retail customers as you identify those who might benefit from your company's products. As you go about your day, listen for opportunities to offer your products to those whom you hear may have a need for them. In network marketing, retailing your products represents one simple way of introducing others to some of the benefits your company offers. Remember that your company's most exciting product is always your income opportunity. Don't sell your opportunity short by failing to offer it to your customers. Recommend the opportunity by showing your plan and inviting others to join you in business daily. Be proud of your opportunity and offer it without attachment, as you would a most precious gift.

3. Sponsor others into your business who see the value of creating a residual income that can contribute to their lives.

BECOME YOUR OWN BEST CUSTOMER

How can you expect others to buy your products or services if you are not a devoted and knowledgeable customer? Replace any competitors' products with your company's offerings. Develop as many product experiences as you can, as you identify your favourite products and what you like so much about them. Speak to others in your company and success line to learn why each product is unique and special. Learn about all the aggressive uses for each and identify any special groups or target markets that each product or service might appeal to. You'll be targeting these groups specifically in your prospecting efforts and with your sales offerings.

GET READY FOR BUSINESS

As a network marketing professional, you'll want to put into place a number of structures and necessities that will allow you to operate your business smoothly and to make a professional impression on your customers and business prospects. Those already in business for themselves will likely have many of these elements already in place. It is important that those just beginning a home business be aware of how vital these support elements are. These include:

1. Get a good, inexpensive long distance phone plan. If your company offers a plan, subscribe to it immediately. If not, look for a plan that charges less than Rs 200 per minute. If you plan on speaking long distance for more than 10 hours per month, an unlimited calling plan may be your best bet.

2. Call your local phone company and subscribe to three-way calling. You'll need this feature to connect your prospects with your success line partners who will be making your business presentations for you until you are able to make your own presentations and support your team to make theirs. Subscribe to your phone company's voice mail or call-answering plan. You will want to leave your prospects and team members with the most professional impression of your business, and an outdated answering machine just won't do. Record a professional and upbeat message to greet your callers with a warm, inviting communication as their first impression.
3. You'll need a toll-free number to remove any reluctance on the part of your customers or prospects calling you back. You can decide if a toll-free number that ties into your local number and rings in your home office will serve you best or if a separate toll-free voice mail will be more convenient for you to use. Some toll-free voice mail companies now offer a follow-me service, whereby you can decide if your calls will forward onto your home, office, or cell phone or go directly to voice mail. Some services allow fax transmission to this same number. Others also allow you the convenience of listening to your messages or reading your faxes as e-mail attachments.
4. If you'll be doing business from different locations, a cell phone will come in handy. Select a plan that suits your usage needs, and make sure you include voice mail and three-way calling with your service.
5. Setup a checking account that you'll use exclusively for your network marketing business. Using an online checkbook or database software programme like Money, Excel, or any other record keeping

system that will allow you to enter all your monthly debits and credits in columns marked to identify the nature of your expense. This will facilitate your record keeping and make for easy computations at the end of each month and at the end of each year in preparation for tax time.

6. In this modern era, if your intentions are to build a network marketing dynasty, a computer is a must. Use it to communicate with your customers, prospects, team members, and company via e-mail, write your letters, and organize your information. You'll also need to send and receive faxes. You can set up your computer to do so or buy a fax/copier/scanner to handle all these functions.
7. Professionals need business cards and labels to communicate the right look and impression. If your company offers these items with their logo, order them there. If not, your local office supply store can create some attractive cards and labels. You can also purchase labels to use with your computer or a separate label-maker attachment. You can create very attractive stationery right on your computer as well. If you decide to print your business cards from your computer, make sure you use quality stock and create a professional appearance.
8. If your company offers an automatic shipping programme, sign up for it to not only receive your products on a regular monthly basis but to also set the proper example for your team. They will do as you do—not as you say. Auto-ship is also a great way to insure you'll never miss a commission check because you forgot to order products that month.
9. If your company offers a duplicable web site, set yours up. Your web site can be a low cost way to

introduce your prospects and display your company's offerings. It also sets another duplicable example for your success team.

10. For those instances when you'll be retailing products or prospecting traditionally (not everyone quite yet is computer literate) order your company's catalogues, prospecting brochures, or audio or videotapes. You'll want to have packages pre-made and on hand at all times so you'll never miss a good prospecting opportunity! Keep a stash readily available in your briefcase, carry bag, car, home, and office.
11. Study all your company's training materials. Learn the value of the compensation plan so you can share its high points enthusiastically. What makes your plan unique and attractive to prospects?
12. Commit to attending all company and success-line sponsored conference calls. If your success-line team or company offers a regularly scheduled opportunity call, commit to listen in and invite at least one guest to three-way call in with you. If training calls are available, listen in while asking questions and taking notes.
13. If your company or success line offers a prerecorded opportunity call, listen in and plan to three-way your prospects. If no such call exists, work with your team to create your own.
14. Get the names and phone numbers of all your upline leaders. Your upline are those people who earn commissions as a result of your efforts, so take advantage of their support. Take the initiative by calling each one to introduce yourself so that you can begin to create a powerful partnership with them. Get to know their strengths and areas of expertise. Request their permission to call on them

for support in building your business. Create a partnership agreement with your upline leaders, those who will be paid on your efforts. You can also use a similar agreement with each of your downline leaders, those individuals whose efforts will result in your own income growth.

15. Create your own story letter, introducing others to your company, products, and opportunity. Your story letter will tell how you were introduced and why you decided to become involved with your company to pursue a the products, the integrity and stability of the company, and the exciting income opportunity available for those who decide to share in the company's profits and growth.
16. Organize your daily schedule and track all of your prospecting, follow-up, and training calls on a daily basis.
17. Create your notification names list. The people on this list are those you will want to notify that you are now in business. Some will become your customers. Others will become your business partners. Others will refer you to new customers and business partners. For whatever reason, others will not be interested in becoming either a customer or a business partner. Do not rule anyone out or prejudge that they would not be interested. You will never know who will be and who will not be open to your offer.

SETTING UP YOUR MASTER PLAN

It's now time for us to speak about the numbers game of network marketing. Speaking with enough people to fill your pipeline with a never-ending stream of interested prospects is critical to achieving success. Coin collectors back then knew for a fact that if they sorted through enough coins, they were sure to find some great gems. All it required was sifting through a sufficient quantity of coins to locate the keepers.

Another example that drives home the sorting process required to be successful in network marketing is the process of shucking oysters. If you open a few oysters, you'll likely find only some grains of sand within their shells. However, if you go through enough to insure your success ratios, you're bound to uncover a bunch containing beautiful and valuable pearls. Knowing that the pearls exist in some of the oyster shells should be enough of a powerful motivator to inspire you to keep at the shucking process until the right prize-containing oysters come along.

Sorting for network marketing leaders works the same way. They are definitely out there, waiting to be discovered by you. Will you speak with enough to have the odds work in your favour? Or will you quit before your pearls are identified? Just as the numbers can work in your favour, if you do not speak with enough people, you'll be much less likely to identify your leaders.

What's more is that with massive, consistent and persistent action, you will generate the momentum needed to attract your prospects to your opportunity. Speaking with one hundred prospects over the course of a week will produce far greater results than speaking with the same hundred over a year's time. Your energy will be different. You'll have so many people to speak with that you will have no time for neediness or desperation in your voice. If you speak only with a few prospects now and then, you'll be more likely to feel a desperate need to get them in. You won't speak with the confidence and unshakable belief required to communicate the rich value and awesome possibilities that await your prospect. After all, beggars don't make very attractive business partners!

4

PROSPECTING NETWORK MARKETING

Network marketing prospecting is arguably the most important skill to master when looking to establish your network marketing business and therefore it is important you invest some time towards developing your technique. Network marketing is essentially a sales and marketing business. The problem with this is that there are very few network marketers who have tertiary qualifications in sales or marketing. Therefore, it is important that you dedicate some of your training time towards learning some basic sales and social marketing principles such that you can develop your prospecting technique.

To start with, one of the biggest mistakes new distributors make in the network marketing industry is to focus purely on recruiting distributors, when what they should be doing is considering a multi-faceted approach which prioritises establishing a solid customer base. Let's look at why?

To understand why network marketing product prospecting is so important we need to quickly review the theory behind network marketing. Network

Marketing is essentially a sales business that uses direct selling and relationship referrals as a method of marketing and selling a company's product line. Individual network marketers act like a franchisee to the parent company and are paid a commission based on the volume of product or services sold as a result of their own organization's efforts.

The key principle we want to emphasis here is that the main goal of any network marketing company is to sell their products or services to the marketplace. Whilst for network marketers, recruiting new distributors can offer numerous attractive bonuses, at the end of the day, moving your company's product (or services) into the marketplace should always take priority over recruiting new distributors (contrary to popular belief). Essentially what we are trying to say is that building a network of customers is the best way to develop a long-term network marketing business and a truly passive income stream.

When network marketing started out over 50 years ago and communication was limited to face-to-face conversations, recruiting distributors was an easy way to find new customers. For example, if you have a current network of 100 people then realistically you are limited to a potential customer base of 100 people, but if you were smart enough to recruit 2 distributors into your downline who also knew 100 people, then you have now expanded your potential market from 100 potential customers to 300 potential customers. In theory this exposes your network marketing company's products to more people and therefore they have a greater potential to profit. Unfortunately one vital step forgotten in this transition is that that network marketers too often focus on expanding their potential customer base instead of expanding their actual customer base.

Whilst some networkers might argue that some compensation plans will pay out different amounts on different levels and therefore there is more incentive to recruit distributors in preference to customers, the reason why some company's choose to do this is to encourage distributors to actively build their business. This will help to establish their potential sales force and therefore facilitate the expansion of their customer base and the movement of their products.

Additionally your upline distributors profit from an expanding customer base. Therefore if they build a downline of active distributors who find customers in theory their customer base will expand exponentially. This concept is one of the driving forces behind the network marketing industry, so where does it go wrong? Why is it that so many new networkers bail out after such a short period? It's actually quite simple, this concept only works if those 100 people actually choose to work (ie find customers).

If you neglect the basic principles of product distribution your network marketing business is sure to struggle over the longer term. Too many new distributors focus their efforts towards recruiting a host of new distributors, when what they should be doing is building a customer base. Don't get us wrong, recruiting distributors will definitely help you to become a successful networker, but, only in the process of actively building a customer base. You can have a whole team distributors but if they fail to find customers, before long your distributors become frustrated at the lack of growth within their business (limited product sales) and they quit. The short term benefits of recruiting distributors have lead to long term frustration as you struggle with downline retention.

PRODUCT PROSPECTING *VS* RECRUITING DISTRIBUTORS

Fact 1. It is easier to find new customers than it is to find new distributors.

Any successful marketer will tell you that it is always easier to find customers than it is to find distributors. Therefore, if you're first starting out, why make it hard for yourself and set yourself up for eventual failure by focusing on recruiting distributors which for many is the hardest thing to do. A smart networker will master the basics first and get some runs on the board by product prospecting and establishing a solid customer base. Building a downline of distributors should come secondary.

Why should we focus on product prospecting?

Firstly, as stated above it's easier to find new customers then recruit distributors. Secondly, it provides an immediate source of income and finally once your prospect has become a customer, your company (if it's a good company) should take care of the rest. Not only are customers easier to find, but there is also less effort required on your behalf to keep customers satisfied then what it takes to recruit and train new distributors. This extra time allows you to focus your efforts towards finding the next customer.

A harsh reality you need to learn (if you haven't already), is that not everybody you speak to will be interested in your business model. In fact, there will be more people that aren't interested in your business opportunity than those who are. This can be very discouraging for new networkers who thought it would be 'easy' to build a business. The most valuable lesson here is that if you limit your prospecting efforts to only those who are interested in your business opportunity, not only are you missing out on a huge market potential, but you risk the long term sustainability and viability of your business. The secret to a successful long term network marketing business is to prioritise building your customer base via product prospecting. Whilst it is important that you also work towards recruiting your frontline distributors, what we are trying to say is that you need to do both. Don't just focus your efforts towards recruiting new distributers and expect them to build your customer base for you.

This is not to say that you shouldn't start recruiting downline distributors from day one, but you need to understand that it is your loyal customer base that will ensure your long-term success and therefore this should be your priority in your new business. Additionally teaching new distributors to build a customer base first is a very duplicable system that helps even new comers to start seeing returns early in their business, which assists in distributor retention, better team moral and enthusiasm. Likewise this customer development activity is the best way to create and sustain momentum in your business.

Remember the people in network marketing with the biggest pay check each week are not necessarily those with the biggest downline, but instead those who make the greatest volume of product sales through their business.

Fact 2. It is easier to convert existing satisfied customers into downline distributors then someone who has had no exposure to your company.

What do you think happens to customers when they try a product that they absolutely love? Naturally, they tell their friends. Although there is no incentive for them to recommend your products, they do anyway. Before long your satisfied customers are referring new customers. Not only does this assist the growth of your customer base, but this also presents you with the perfect opportunity to discuss your business opportunity with those referring customers, such that you can get them on board as a distributor. "If you're so good at referrals you should be rewarded for it.... welcome to network marketing!"

There are numerous benefits to building an active customer base in your network marketing business in which we have only briefly highlighted a few. The good news is you're never too late to start.

NETWORK MARKETING PRODUCT TRAINING

The marketing mix uses 4 P's to help you understand the marketability of your product.

- *Product*—What are you selling?
- *Price*—What does it cost?
- *Placement*—What locations can your product be purchased?
- *Promotion*—How will your consumers find out about your product?

Most good network marketing companies have already done their homework and designed a generic marketing mix strategy for their distributors to use. However, understanding this basic process can help you to better position yourself into the market place, expand your customer base and increase your product sales.

First, let's explore the 4 P's that make up the marketing mix and discuss how we can improve the marketability your network marketing products.

Product

Your product is a profitable item (or service) that offers a solution to a consumer's need/want/desire. A very valuable lesson in network marketing product training is that your goal should not be to sell a want/need/desire, but instead offer a solution for a problem (want/need/desire) that already exists. In business we don't create a problem; we simply have to develop a strategy to respond to what's already there.

Price (and the value proposition)

The price generally refers to the monetary cost associated with your product (or service), however we would like to extend this definition to include the value gained by the customer for using your company's product (e.g. branding, quality, product experience, practicality etc.). When developing a marketing strategy for your product it is a good idea to consider the cost/value ratio of your product. For example, at your local supermarket you will find many different varieties of bread. While some people are happy to buy the cheap "no brand" product others are willing to spend more for a brand they trust or a product that they believe delivers better value (e.g. flavour, health benefits, shelf life etc).

To look at it another customers don't just buy products or services, they by benefits, or bundles of benefits. Understanding the cost/value ratio of your product can help you to tailor your marketing campaign to specific consumers that would actively be looking for such benefits.

One of the advantages of network marketing is that it allows you to develop a strong relationship with your customers, adding to the value of their product experience.

Placement

The placement refers to the location in which your product can be purchased. In general, the more conveniently your product is placed for your target market to access, the more likely you are to make a sale.

Placement should also be considered in the overall cost/value ratio of your product as discussed above. For example your local corner shop is generally more expensive then the big brand supermarkets, but if you're only going to buy milk, the placement and the cost/value ratio tends to lean in favour of your local corner shop when you take in consideration travel time, parking, queue waiting times, customer service, convenience etc.

One way that network marketing companies have tried to make their products more conveniently located in the marketplace is through direct selling, which allows the consumer to establish a direct relationship with the manufacturer. Advances in communication and technology continue to make this process even more convenient where consumers are now able to place and change orders over the internet.

Whilst for the younger, internet savvy generation this offers good product placement and convenience, it is also important to understand that not everybody has confidence in their ability to use the internet and therefore being able to use the phone (or meet with someone face to face) may offer some consumers a more desirable option.

Promotion

To properly understand promotion it is best if we initially think big picture and then work towards being more specific for your network marketing business. Promotion has 4 distinct elements – advertising (paid advertising for example TV, radio, posters etc), public relations (which is basically non-paid advertising eg editorials, winning awards, presentations, testimonials etc.), word of mouth (relationship referrals - traditional networking approach) and point of sale (were the transaction occurs). Whilst most network marketing companies rely on the word of mouth approach, do not feel that you should be limited to this. There is no single magic bullet in regards to promotion and therefore a combination of strategies is most likely to achieve the greatest results.

When you put the 4 p's together the ideal message to promote your products to your target market is:

Promotional Message: We have a great product in response to your problem (need/want/desire) at a wonderful price (cost/value ratio), which is conveniently placed (easily accessible).

Now obviously you don't have to say it like this, but this is essentially what you want your target audience to be thinking in response to any product marketing campaign. If you can do this, making a product sale should be easy.

Whilst there are 4 p's that make up the traditional marketing mix, there are a few additional P's that we believe should also be considered when developing the ideal marketing strategy and these include:

The competent person (essentially this refers to you and your downline members) who interacts with the potential customer and is able to tailor their product solution towards the customer's problem (need/want / desire).

The physical evidence that you product (or service) provides good value and will satisfy their need/want/ desire. Good examples include a product demonstrations, product testimonials, being able to sample the product etc.

The pleasure that your customer receives as a result of purchasing your product (i.e. customer satisfaction). This does not only include the satisfaction of the product itself but also the friendly service and the future customer care that they receive to keep them loyal.

HOW TO FIND NETWORK MARKETING CUSTOMERS?

The main difference between a network marketing business and your traditional business model is that unlike your standard shoe shop in a supermarket where there is always traffic walking past the shop window to see what you have for sale, in network marketing people do not know what you have for sale unless you show or conversationally promote/recommend them. A very simple fact in business is that no-one is going to buy a product or join a business if they do not know it exists. Where in traditional business models customers generally come to you because they have seen what you have for sale or been influenced by an advert or promotion, in a network marketing business, until you have a solid customer base, you need to be proactive in finding your network marketing customers by taking your product and positioning yourself in the marketplace.

Regardless of whether you are trying to promote your product or your business solution, your goal is to identify your prospects 'problem' and then tailor your solution to be specific to their requirements. Additionally you should always put the customer's needs first, that is, think of how you can help them instead of how much they can help you (ie profiting from the sale).

Let's look at an example.

Let's assume that you are trying to find network marketing customers for your skin care range and that you have setup a product stand at an expo. Someone (prospect) approaches your product stand, how should you respond?

Instead of blatantly trying to promote the first product you can get your hands on, the best approach would be to politely greet your prospect and then try to identify your prospects need/want/desire (problem), such that you can potentially solve it. For example, you might consider asking the following question after your greeting:

"Are you looking for anything in particular?"

This is a simple leading question that can help to qualify your prospect and or identify their need/want/desire early in the conversation. After asking this question your prospect will respond by either revealing their problem (need/want/desire) or with something like "just looking" in which case both are positive responses. You now in some cases have already indentified a need/want/desire and for those who have responded "just looking" you have now set yourself up to ask a follow up question:

"Do you have any particular skin care concerns, in which I might be able to offer some advice?"

This is great prospect qualifying question as they are required to think about their need/want/desire and if they don't offer it, then there is a fair chance that they were never interested in your products in which case you can simply respond by saying:

"Please let me know if you need help or more information on anything."

This now allows you to concentrate your efforts towards prospecting others and also invites them to chase you if they change their mind.

The person asking the questions is always the person in control of a conversation and therefore learning to ask the right questions can go a long way to helping you establish network marketing customers.

Physical Evidence Works Best

An additional word of advice regarding your product prospecting technique is that while facts tell, stories sell. When approaching your prospects to promote your products or services, if you refer to the facts or features you will generally be perceived as a sales-person (ok in some situations). On the other hand if you can provide an example (physical evidence e.g. testimonial) as to how your products have helped someone to overcome a given situation (i.e. products provide benefit in solving a problem) your prospects will be more open to hear what you have to offer.

How to Promote Your Products and Find Network Marketing Customers?

There are basically 4 ways in which you can find network marketing customers for your business. Each method uses a slightly different approach and while initially it is probably best to focus on the method in which you feel most comfortable with, in the long term it a combination of all strategies is likely to achieve the greatest results.

- Casual Prospecting Network
- Marketing Product Display
- Network Marketing Product Parties
- Network Marketing Advertising

Casual Prospecting

Network marketing casual prospecting is arguably the most important skill you can master in your network marketing business as it does not require you to invest a great deal of your time or money. If delivered correctly, this relationship referral method is a very effective, non-invasive marketing technique that every network marketer can feel comfortable with.

Casual prospecting refers to being able to recommend your products and promote their related benefits (or business) in normal everyday conversation, not because you were intentionally looking to prospect the person you are talking to, but because they have presented you with a perfect opportunity to promote what you have to offer.

Breaking the Network Marketing Stereotype

People often form a stereotype that network marketers look for an opportunity to prospect every person that they meet, this is definitely not the norm and we strongly encourage otherwise. There are however conversions that you may have every day that often presents you with the perfect opportunity to casually prospect. It's up to you as to whether you choose to capitalise on them.

Before we take you through the casual prospecting process, let's recap an important marketing concept. A product is a profitable item that offers a solution to a consumer's need/want /desire. One of the most valuable lessons you can learn in marketing is that your goal should not be to sell a problem (want/need / desire), but instead offer a solution for a problem that already exists.

In business we don't create a problem we simply have to develop a strategy to respond to what's already there.

In network marketing one of the key principles to success is being able to indentify your prospect's problem and then being able to tailor your solution to meet your prospect's requirements.

The art of casual prospecting allows you to recommend your products as a solution to a problem that has already been offered by your prospect in normal conversation. For example, if you market health and wellness products and were talking to someone who was suffering from a common cold or hay fever this might present you with the opportunity to do some casual prospecting. Please note in this example below how the message is conveyed via a personal testimonial or a story.

"I used to suffer really bad hay fever as well, but since I've been taking these supplements I've felt fantastic, you might want to give them a try?"

If they respond with a 'No thanks', change the conversation. Remember professionals sort, amateurs convince. If the answer is 'Yes', great you've almost certainly made the sale, at this point don't go on and on about how good the products are and what cutting-edge science is behind them (as your prospect will then ask themselves what your motives are – to help them or to sell them); instead revert back to a normal conversation. At the end of the conversation collect their details, such that you can follow-up and organize for them to trial or use the products.

Do not make misleading claims about your products or services. You can not only get yourself in a lot of trouble, but you may also be doing your company a disservice as well. While it is ok to give truthful product testimonials and to say that a given product helped you (or another) to deal with a given problem, you cannot promote a product as a proven solution unless there is concrete evidence to support your claim.

Incidentally the example used above is a true story. I personally used to suffer really bad hay fever and would spend a large sum of money to help prevent and control this using medication. After trying a product referred to me by a friend I found almost instant improvement in my condition and as a result I have now been taking this product for several years. Whilst to this day I still don't know what ingredient improves my hay fever, I don't have too, all I need to say is that it's provided tangible benefits for me.

Casual Prospecting the Right Way

So what is the most effective approach to use when casually prospecting? Generally, the best approach is to provide your solution in the form of physical evidence (eg testimonials) of how your products or services have helped you (or someone else) to deal with the identified problem such as that used in the example above. Alternatively if you don't have a testimonial of how your products helped to solve that specific problem, you can use a testimonial of how your products helped to solve somebody else's (unrelated) problem and that maybe it could also help them.

For example if somebody presents to you with a common cold you might casually prospect by saying:..."I know what it's like to feel sick, I used to suffer really bad hay fever, but since I've been taking these supplements, I've felt fantastic. Maybe they could also help you with your cold? You might want to give them a try? "

The right approach reinforces that your prospect has a problem and that you have a possible solution, inviting your prospect to act accordingly. If your initial statement sparks interest but isn't enough to make the sale, let your marketing tools (e.g. Product brochures etc) do the work for you. For example, if your prospect requests 'more information', you're generally best not to try and sell your product by going into the finer details. Instead offer to take their details such that you can forward them some product information. Naturally this prospecting process would be continued by a friendly follow up call to show your concern and see if the information helped.

Three key tips to remember here are:

— 'Less is more' – Wait for the opportunity and then deliver your message briefly in the form of a testimonial or story, but don't go into a sell.

— Swap details at the end of the conversation or ask permission to get back in touch with the person with some further information regarding their problem or need.

— Don't forget to follow-up, as there is nothing more unprofessional than offering to help someone and then not following through.

Casual Prospecting the Wrong Way

The inexperienced networker is often tempted to provide too much information about their products or present it in a way that deters even the most motivated prospects. "Have I got a solution for you, these vitamins are the best...etc." This blatant sell technique normally results in your prospects responding "No thanks" and you left wondering what went wrong?!

The Ideal Casual Prospecting Situation

Another way to casually prospect is to become a 'product of your product'. There is no better product promoting opportunity in network marketing then when somebody notices something about you and wants to know your solution, providing you with the perfect opportunity to recommend your product.

Let's use weight loss as an example. If you're company has a weight loss programme and you need to lose weight, why not make a conscious effort to go through the programme yourself, such that when you bump into someone in the street and they see your success (physical evidence that your product works), they will want to hear about your solution. This provides you with the perfect opportunity to promote your product.

There is no better prospecting opportunity as that of when somebody approaches you for a solution. The best way to put yourself in this position is to become a product of your product.

Network Marketing Product Display

The network marketing product display is one of the many ways to promote your products and help build your network marketing customer base.

The network marketing product display method as the names suggests involves creating a visual display of the products that you are trying to market and then positioning it in a location that it is likely to have consumer traffic.

Examples of a Network Marketing Product Display may include:

- Stall at the markets
- Adjunct to a primary business (e.g. hairdressing business who then has a beauty product or shampoo display in their shop)
- Expo or Presentation stand (e.g. a network marketing product stand placed within a theme related expo or at a product related presentation.)
- Product parties
- In store promotions/on-site product display's
- Information stands providing information about the products (if it is not possible to display products or services)

The network marketing product display method if done correctly is a good way of marketing your product to a broad range of potential customers. The advantage of this approach is that any person who willingly approaches a product display is already curious to find out more and therefore open to being approached by the sales representative. Bearing this in mind, the very first step to creating a successful network marketing product display is to make it visually appealing. This doesn't mean you need to have all the bells and whistles, but it should look professional and inviting.

Tips to Making a Good Network Marketing Product Stand:

- Visually appealing
- Some other way of attracting customers (e.g. competition entry, giveaway lollies etc.)

– Appropriately dressed assistant (i.e. dressed appropriately for the occasion and surroundings).

– Having someone who is personable and capable of building rapport with your prospective customer, but not pushy or fake in trying to push for a sale. This person should be capable of identifying the prospective customer's needs and also be familiar with benefits of the products. Additionally this person should be able to relate relevant testimonials.

– Provide an incentive to order or purchase now (i.e. save 15% if you order today or purchase today and go into the draw for ....), alternatively have take home information for those who can't purchase on the spot and provide an incentive if they order in the next few days.

– Have a way of collecting contact details of interested parties or potential customers (e.g. surveys and competition entry forms).

  Note: If you intend to collect peoples contact details for the purpose for contacting them at a later date, ensure that they give consent for you to do so.

Where Should I Set Up My Network Marketing Product Display?

One of the best places to position your network marketing product display is in amongst other theme related products (or services), as you are likely to attract more qualified customers. If customers are interested in other similar products or services, then there is fair chance they will also be interested in what you have to offer. For example if you have a health product a good place to set up a product display or stand would be at a Health and Fitness expo, as the majority of people attending the expo will already be interested in health related products.

This helps to explain why you will find a number of similar theme related stores in the one place. For example, you might find 4 or 5 fast food chains within walking distance of one another, a street full of car detailers, or perhaps a strip of clothing shops. Conventional thinking would have you believe that this is a bad strategy as they would be working in competition to one another, but in fact this is actually (not always) a smart marketing strategy as you are positioning yourself in a location that already attracts qualified customers who are looking for your kind of products or services.

Tips to Improve Your Network Marketing Product Sales

Consumers look for physical evidence that a product works and therefore where possible you should look to capitalise on this concept. Depending on what product your company markets you might like to try some of the following:

- *Sample some of the product*–This works particular well for products that appeal to the senses, for example if you sell a hand cream that smells good and feels great to run through your hands, the best way to capitalise on this would be to let your customers sample it (onsite), as the product will sell itself.
- *Product demonstration*–If they can't sample it, then show them how it works. Note: Your demonstration should be quick and easy with your customers thinking 'I can do that'. If your product takes a long time to demonstrate or is complex you might be better off to skip the demonstration.
- *Testimonials*–If there is one thing better than a testimonial it's a variety of testimonials. If you're just starting out, use the generic celebrity testimonials that your company uses and contact

your upline to ask if you can use some of theirs. Ideally as your customer base grows you can collect a whole folder full of testimonials from 'everyday people' that your customers can flick through to convince themself why they should empty their wallets.

— *Money back guarantee* – Basically says 'no risk' to the customer. Most network marketing company's now offer money back guarantees with their products so if this is applicable to your business we suggest you use this to your advantage. It shouldn't be the most visible statement at your product stand (looks like a tacky infomercial), but it should be there to easily refer to, if you need help to get your customers over the line.

In summary the network marketing product display if done correctly can be a very effective and fun way to attract and interact with your customers. Whilst we always recommend that you take your business seriously, remember you don't necessarily have to take yourself seriously. You'd be surprised how attractive a little fun can be.

Network Marketing Product Parties

Whilst Network Marketing Product Parties were traditionally seen as an old school method of direct selling, today they are back in fashion and more popular than ever. If done correctly product parties offer one of the most time efficient methods of making product sales and in establishing a loyal customer base.

Network marketing product parties have been around for many years and have consistently shown to be one of the easiest ways to find new customers. So what's different, why the recent surge in popularity?

Traditionally product parties were used to sell non-consumable items (e.g. Tupperware, clothing, jewellery etc.) that offered little or no incentive for customers to provide any extra or repeat business. Therefore to make good money distributors we're required to continually hold parties, or recruit new distributors to leverage their efforts. More recently smart networkers with consumable products (e.g. skin care, beauty products, candles etc.) have learnt to capitalise on the success of those before them and realized the massive potential with the benefit of repeat business (and profits) from their new customers for little or no extra work. Additionally, many of modern day network marketing products require the customer to gain personal hands on experience of the product before they are likely to purchase, making parties the ideal product promoting environment.

Essentially the modern day network marketing product parties present the ideal environment to find new customers. The main advantage to marketing a consumable product is that once have to provided an excellent or unique first time customer experience, it is usually simply a matter of plugging them into your customer care programme such that they keep coming back for repeat business.

Whoever originally thought of product parties is a marketing genius. One of the most important steps to making any sale is to make your customer feel comfortable. Using the product party method your potential customers (usually women) are surrounded by friends and family in a comfortable, fun, casual environment, where they knowingly attend the party to be influenced by the sales representative. This presents the ideal product prospecting environment. Not only does your host attract all the customers, but there are usually incentives for the host to facilitate sales. Win – Win!!

People often assume that product parties do not offer the return required to generate a full time income and that you have to be continually holding parties to see a return. This is usually because people forget to factor in repeat business. The aim is not just to find new customers but also turn these people into repeat customers. If you have a good product, then all it takes is a few successful parties and an effective customer care programme and your well on your way to establishing a loyal customer base.

Tips to Holding a Network Marketing Product Party:

— Consider your product (not all products will make for good parties–i.e. providers of telecommunications services).

— As soon as you book a party get your host to start sending out invitations straight away, don't leave them to the last minute.

— Offer incentives for the host if they provide a large audience. It is generally best to over invite by at least 25%, as there will generally be people who cannot attend or are no-shows on the day. Additionally buying is contagious so when a few seem interested this can easily filter through the rest of the group.

— After you have booked a party remember to confirm at least twice, provide some incentive for people to come (e.g. a free small sample or inexpensive gift).

— Look for ways to enhance your party prospects experience (i.e. games, trivia, prizes etc.)

— Where possible create a relaxed atmosphere and enhance the prospects mood by providing sensory enhancement (appropriate lighting, music etc.).

— Where possible let your products sell themselves, ie a quick explanation / demonstration and then give your prospects hands on experience. This works extremely well with skincare and beauty products as they can see, smell, feel the response (physical evidence that your product has value).

- Consider the language that you use when describing your products. You don't have to know every little detail about your product but you should consider using describing words that make your product appeal to the audience.
- Support demonstrations with personal or third party testimonials.
- Provide some incentive for people to purchase at the party or to place an order (e.g. save 10%, purchase today and receive a free gift or get 3 for the price 2 if you order today).
- Follow-up to get feedback on your new customer's experience. This is also an opportune time to get some referrals and to encourage them to make another purchase and/or provide them with some information that value-ads to their customer experience.

If you're new to holding network marketing product parties, we strongly encourage you to arrange an on-the-job training run with an experienced distributor.

Network Marketing Advertising

Network marketing advertising allows individual distributors to develop lead generation campaigns that if done correctly can provide a large number of pre-qualified leads in which distributors can then convert into valuable customers or downline distributors

Whilst marketing campaigns are generally considered by most small businesses to require an element of skill and planning to ensure that you receive a return on your investment, this should not deter those with little or no marketing or advertising experience, but instead encourage those interested to do some extra reading to ensure that your time and money are well invested.

For many new to networking, advertising is often seen as being the least confronting way of build a business, however it can also be the most frustrating if the time and money invested provides little or no return. Therefore a network marketing advertising campaign should be considered adjunct to other customer building strategies and not as the only strategy to build your business.

When developing a marketing campaign it is important that you have some form of 'how to' guide that can assist you to step through the necessary processes.

PROFESSIONAL PROSPECTING

Professional prospecting is all about learning to take a professional approach to your prospecting. This method, if done correctly, will significantly improve your rate of success and therefore we strongly recommend all network marketers to invest some time into developing their prospecting technique.

Network marketing is a sales business, the problem with this is that the main reason people join a network marketing company is not to sell anything, but instead to improve their quality of life. So how do you sell a product if you don't want to become a salesperson? One approach is to sell yourself, not your product.

Pre-selling and Pre-Qualifying your Prospects

One of the most proven methods of establishing a network marketing business is to focus not so much on the selling of your products to your prospects, but instead to concentrate on the pre-selling of yourself and the pre-qualifying of your prospects such that you can identify how to let your products or business model sell themselves.

The professional prospecting approach involves two steps:

- — Building a relationship with your prospects so you understand their needs and wants whilst earning their trust and respect (pre-selling yourself).
- — requalifying your prospect to see if they have the qualities you are looking for to join your business or the desire to purchase your type of products.

The advantage of this approach is that you are holding all the cards. You have complete control over whether your prospects are worthy of hearing the opportunity you have to offer. Essentially if your prospects don't meet your selection criteria then you don't have to try and proceed with the sale.

One of the best pieces of advice we can offer anybody who is starting out in a network marketing business is to take a professional prospecting approach. A good distinction to remember is that—Professionals sort, amateurs convince.

Amateur network marketers treat every lead as a customer and try to convince them why they should become a customer\or business owner and as a result are rejected more times than not. Professional networkers sort their prospects and only target those who have the qualities they are looking for and as a result have a much greater success rate. Prequalifying your prospects is a very important step of the professional prospecting process and should not be overlooked.

How to Pre-sell your Prospects?

One of the most important concepts to remember when developing your professional prospecting technique is that the main reason people join a network marketing company is to improve their quality of life. Therefore to successfully make a sale you have to offer something that is of value to others or have something that people want.

Having the Right Attitude

To start with, let us focus on some basic psychology. In particular a quality in someone's personality that appeals to everyone—happiness. Everyone wants to enjoy life and people are quick to pick up positive energy. If you present yourself as a positive person that is happy and appears to be enjoying life, people will admire your personal qualities and they will be willing to do what you do in order to have what you have. Prospects will always buy into your persona first and therefore professional prospecting requires you to get the basics right and have the right attitude.

Let's look at an example: If you have just listened to somebody's sob story for the last 30 mins and then they try to tell you about this "fantastic" opportunity. What are your initial thoughts?

Probably something along the lines of—if it's so fantastic, why are they so miserable? It does not matter how good the opportunity is, most prospects will have already made up their mind before they even get a chance to review it.

The good news is that the opposite is also true. If you present yourself to be happy and enjoying life your prospects will be more open to review what you have to offer. Essentially the point we are trying to make is that presenting yourself with a positive attitude and the right approach can significantly improve your rate of prospecting success as it helps to pre-sell your prospect.

Personal Appearance

When prospecting, you want to leave the person with a good impression and so we encourage you to take pride in your personal appearance. Stand tall and be proud of who you are and what you do. Additionally, it is important that you smile and be excited to meet your prospects. This becomes even more important if you are working in the health and wellness industry, or with fashion or beauty products. This is not to say that you need to look like a supermodel, but if you are trying to convince someone that you have the keys to a multimillion dollar business and/or the best products available, we recommend that you take a professional approach and dress appropriately.

An easy way to set yourself up for professional prospecting success is to dress smart, take pride in your appearance and become a product of your product. A basic sales tip to remember is that while facts tell, stories sell. If your prospects can see that you look and feel great as a result of your products they won't be able to get their hands on your products quick enough.

Building a Relationship

Successful network marketers often refer to the industry as "relationship marketing" because one of the key principles to professional prospecting is in the relationships you build with your prospects. If your prospects know, like and trust you, they will be more willing to listen to what you have to share. Essentially if you are asking a prospect to join your downline, you first have to establish a relationship where this prospect would feel comfortable working with you. Taking the time to build a relationship with your prospects can definitely help you to convert them into customers or downline distributors. An easy guideline to remember when talking with your prospects is that you should always aim to create friends first.

Identify your Prospects Hot Buttons

Getting to know your prospects, more specifically their wants, needs and problems can help you to tailor your business solution towards the individual. Ultimately you need to learn how your business opportunity or products could improve your prospects quality of life. These factors are more commonly known in the industry as "hot buttons". They are the motivating incentives that will promote a prospect to take action. Getting to know and understand a prospect's hot buttons gives you an opportunity to offer a solution. Remember, not everyone is in it for the money.

When speaking to a fresh prospect or lead, remember your initial goal should always be to build a relationship first. A good way to do this is to ask questions and listen to what they have to say. Taking an interest in your prospect's lives will not only assist you to establish your relationship, but it will also help to identify their hot buttons. This will eventually create an opening for you to present your opportunity.

In summary, professional prospecting requires you to give the impression that you are a positive person and your life is full of fun and enjoyment. Be interested in what your prospects have to say, show that you care and that you are supportive of your fellow colleagues. Ask questions of your prospects and listen to what they have to say, devoting 100% of your attention toward your prospects.

Even if you're meeting with people that you have known for years, or if you're talking to people on the phone, smile, be positive and present yourself to be happy and to be enjoying life. These people will notice your behaviour and want to know the secret to your recent happiness.

Additionally, your professional prospecting goal isn't just to build a relationship with your prospects, but also to pre-qualify them. An easy way to begin the prequalifying process is that once you have established a relationship, you should then be asking yourself the following questions:

- Could I improve this prospect's quality of life with my products?
- If yes, how? What hot buttons have they provided?
- Does this person have the qualities I'm looking for to join my business?
- If yes, how can I present my opportunity such that it offers a solution to their problems, or improves their quality of life?

In particular, when it comes to finding downline distributors your goal is to find the right people, not just the willing. Essentially you are looking for motivated, teachable people who will actively work your business for you.

At this point it is probably important to emphasise that not everyone you know or speak to will have the qualities that you are looking for. In this situation you are best to cut your losses, enjoy the fact that you have just made a new friend and be willing to walk away. Don't feel that you have to sell to everyone you speak with, as before too long, people will see you coming and walk the other way. Remember professionals sort, amateurs convince. As a professional your goal is simply to build relationships and then identify (pre-qualify) those who may benefit from what you have to offer. If your prospects meet the criteria you are looking for, great, the next step is to continue to build the relationship and look for the most ideal opening to present your opportunity.

Once you have prequalified your prospects and identified their hot buttons, it is important that you don't jump at the first chance to share what you have to offer. Be patient and continue to build your relationship as good things come to those who wait. Jumping in too early can easily undo your groundwork and weaken the trust that you have created in your relationship.

HOW TO BUILD A DOWNLINE?

Every successful networker knows that in order to build a downline of distributors you have to be actively presenting your prospects with your business opportunity, and while this is not rocket science, the way in which you approach it can significantly alter the outcomes. So what is the best way to present your business opportunity?

Network marketing is essentially a sales and marketing business. The problem with this is that there are very few network marketers that have tertiary qualifications in sales and/or marketing. Therefore, one of the most effective techniques to building your downline is to a take slightly different, but highly effective and simple approach.

Share the business opportunity, don't sell it

The concept of sharing the business opportunity basically means that your primary goal is get your prospects to look at some information and then let someone else (eg upline distributor) or something else (e.g. prospecting tool) do the selling for you. For example, in response to their hot button you may choose to invite them along to a business opportunity presentation which might help to solve their problems, alternatively you may give someone a DVD to watch or refer them to an online presentation.

In recent years there have been a number of advances within the network marketing industry and in particular the development of prospecting tools, which has made sharing your network marketing business easy and more time efficient. Some examples may include:

- DVD presentations
- Online presentations
- Local Business Opportunity Meetings

- Live Webcasts – Presentations broadcast live over the internet
- Publications -newspapers, magazines etc.
- Company websites
- Audio presentations

The main benefit to using such prospecting tools is that it takes you out of the sales role, allowing professionally made sales tools or successful upline distributors to do all the hard work for you. Additionally you do not have to spend countless hours researching your products and business model as the prospecting tools will generally answer all of the questions for you. Win-win.

Using this downline building technique, your primary prospecting goal is simply to get to some information in their hand and an idea in their head. Anymore than a 30 second summary and an invitation to review some information is probably too much. The aim is to keep your approach brief and allow your prospecting tool to do the work.

After reviewing the information, your prospects are either interested to know more or they are not. Your prospects are now fully qualified and you know which ones to pursue. Are there any lost friends or hard feelings using this technique? No, because as far as they are concerned you didn't try to sell them anything. They presented to you with a problem or an area of their life that could be improved and all you did was offer them a 'possible' solution. Those who are interested will want to know more, whereas those who aren't interested won't.

Don't ever dismiss a prospect even though they may have initially turned you down. It is human nature to fear the unknown. If you are just starting out in the business as far as your prospects are concerned you haven't been in the business long enough to know what the future holds. Go back to them in 6 months. After seeing your success they may be more willing to look at what you have to offer.

Don't get us wrong, although we refer to this process as 'sharing' the information you are in fact selling, but the difference here is that you are taking a strategic approach by trying to promote some information that may be of relevance, as opposed to blatantly trying to sell your business. If after reviewing the information your prospects are interested to take the next step, they have essentially sold themselves.

Throughout the entire business prospecting process your ultimate goal is to have your prospects walk away with a commitment to either review some material (prospecting tool) or attend a meeting or presentation. This is best achieved through building a relationship with your prospects and through identifying their hot buttons such that you can then offer them your solution.

If your prospects start to ask questions immediately after you have delivered your information it is important to remember that your goal is to share the information, not to sell your opportunity. That's what the tools are for. Therefore a good response to any question is to refer them back to the tool/appointment that you have just provided for them.

"That's a great question and everything will be explained in the...... (tool provided/ appointment). How about I give you a call on....... (follow up date) and we can go through any questions then? "

The follow up is arguably the most important aspect to converting your prospects into downline distributors and we will discuss this in more detail later. At this point however it is important to emphasise that when you deliver a prospecting tool you must also remember to arrange a convenient time to follow up to see if they are interested in knowing more. One of the biggest mistakes a new Network Marketer makes is in creating an interest with a prospect, but then not effectively following-up.

One final point to consider when using this downline building technique is that given you are relying on your prospecting tools to do the selling for you, it is important that you get to know each of your prospecting tools such that you can tailor your approach to meet your prospects needs. While some prospects might enjoy the convenience of the internet, others might prefer to watch a DVD. Do not overwhelm your prospects and give them too much information or homework to do as this approach can deter even the most motivated of people.

The role of the initial prospecting tool is to spark interest, not to explain every minor detail about your products or company. If after reviewing the initial information they want to know more, great, you have got them interested. Provide them with the necessary information and get one of your upline sponsors to help you close the deal and convert them to downline distributor.

Although prospecting tools are a great way to share your business opportunity and help build your downline, the way in which they are delivered and followed up on is important. Do not ever try to force information upon your prospects. As discussed previously, the best approach is to build the relationship first such that they are open to hear what you have to share. If your prospects are reluctant to accept your information, maintain you dignity, respect their decision, withdraw the information and change the topic of conversation. Remember professionals sort, amateurs convince. Reality is that you can't win every prospect and trying to do so will only disrupt your potential friendships and damage your reputation. This helps to explain why pre-qualifying is so important.

PREPARING THE FOLLOW UP

The follow up is the most important part of the prospecting process, therefore a little bit of thought and time should be dedicated to ensure you are well prepared.

Sifting and Sorting *vs* Convincing

Although we have briefly touched on this point before, now is a good time to reemphasise it. When you are moving your prospect through the prospecting formulae, do not be afraid to disqualify the person from your business opportunity if they do not have the qualities you are looking for. Remember, you are looking for the right people not just the willing. The right people are those who will go to work for you, they are self-motivated and have the potential to become leaders. Those who are willing but lack motivation are more than likely going to provide you with short term gratification but long tern frustration as they fail to get their businesses properly established.

Additionally, do not be afraid of your prospect saying no. They are not rejecting you, they are rejecting the product or the business. More often than not the timing isn't right or they are uncertain of how they will go. Even if your prospects aren't interested you should always remain friendly with them and finish by saying that you will let them know how you go as this will then give you the opportunity to approach them again at a later date.

It is critical that you understand that we are in the sifting and sorting business, not the convincing business. You want your prospect to be completely comfortable with the entire prospecting process. Do not be afraid to ask if your prospect feels comfortable throughout the conversation and always ask your prospect for permission to call them back or to send them more information. This will automatically build respect with your prospect as they can see that you value their time and privacy.

Edification

When you are first starting out in network marketing we encourage you to get an experienced upline distributor (mentor/expert) to assist you when prospecting and more importantly during the follow up. If you are meeting with someone for the follow up, bringing along a more experienced team member will improve your conversion rate. It is always a good idea to inform your prospects that you intend to bring along an experienced colleague to the meeting to help answer any of their questions. If you are following up with a phone call, having your experienced upline join you in a three way call works just as effectively.

If you intend to use this strategy it is important that you speak highly of your colleague and their achievements because this will help your prospects gain respect for them. This process is known as edification and has been a critical factor that has driven the success of the network marketing industry for many years. This edification process should be included as part of all network marketers initial training, as it allows on the-job training and the ability to learn first-hand how to improve your prospecting technique. The following diagram helps to summarise this process.

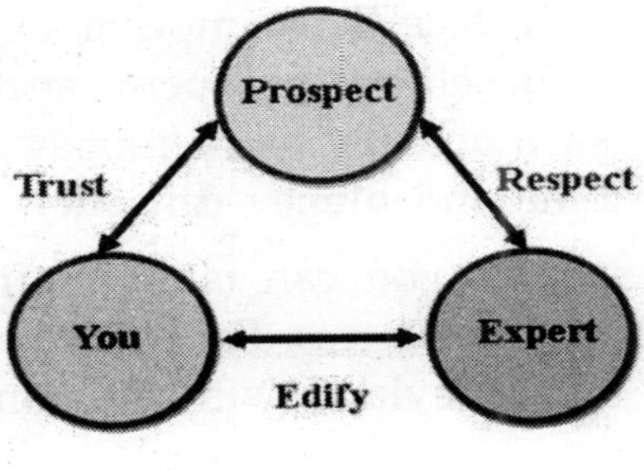

The relationship you build with your prospect creates an element of trust, and through edifying your business colleagues, your prospect gains respect for them and values what they have to say. Allowing your prospects to witness this supportive network first-hand can be a significant selling factor that triggers them to take action.

What are you trying to sell?

At this point it is also important that we recap on basic marketing principles. Unless you are trying to convert existing network marketers, your prospects aren't looking for a good compensation plan or the 'best products', they are simply looking for a solution to their existing problems and this where your focus should be. You're selling a solution, not a product. A good example of this is the person who goes to the local hardware store to buy a ¼ inch drill, essentially what they are looking for is a ¼ inch hole. The drill is simply a solution to solving their problem.

What we are trying to say is that at the end of the day it doesn't matter how good the compensation plan is, or even the product line, if you can sell the solution, the method (business vehicle) shouldn't matter. Having said this we strongly encourage networkers to partner with a network marketing company that is ethical, has integrity and a good track record.

When trying to sell a business model most networkers assume that their prospects will buy into it because it can offer them more money and /or more time. While this is partly true, it is important that you tailor your solution to be client (prospect) specific. In other words it's not so much the extra money and time, but what the extra time and money can offer them.

The more specific you can tailor your solution, the greater your chance of success. For example, the ability to take that trip to Disneyland with the family that they have always wanted, the dream house that they are so close to getting, the desire to open their own coffee shop etc. This is why getting to know your prospect in the prequalifying stage is so important. The best approach is when you can use their 'own words' in the solution. Before approaching your prospect for the follow up you should be asking yourself the following question:

What key emotional phrases (hot buttons) has this prospect given me, which I can use to tailor my solution?

Leadership

One final point to remember before approaching the follow up (and prospecting process in general) is that you need to believe 100% in yourself, your business and in your solution. You can expect your prospects to ask you questions and throw you objections, so if you don't fully believe in what you are doing then your prospects will see right through you. The biggest selling factor in network marketing is leadership. If this person is going to work alongside you, they need to be assured that you are confident about what you are doing and not have any reservations. If you can prove yourself to be a leader your prospects will follow.

CLOSING THE DEAL

Closing the deal is one of the most satisfying achievements in any business, particularly network marketing and therefore learning to improve your closure technique is a good investment.

To try and simplify the closing the deal process we have created a simple two step process that you should consider when contacting you're prospects to discuss their response to the initial information you provided them.

- Continue to develop the relationship, and
- The sales pitch

Step 1. Developing the relationship

Firstly, when ever meeting or phoning your prospect to conduct the follow up it is important that you continue to build rapport with that person, as you don't want to give the impression that you are just trying to sell them something. A good way to do this is to ask them questions about things you have learnt about them during the relationship building stage of the prospecting process. For example, if you learnt that they were going to see a football game, ask them about the game; if one of their kids (best if you can remember their name) had a star role in the school play, ask them about the play etc.

This relationship building phase is a very important step towards closing the deal as your prospect will always be more receptive towards you if you have taken an active interest in them. People love to talk about themselves, so if you can show that you listened and were interested in what they were saying in your previous encounters, you have gone a long way towards creating a winning relationship. This step also develops an aspect of trust from your prospect that would enable them, if they so choose to join your business, to feel comfortable in coming to you for advice.

The next step to successfully closing the deal is to approach the sale. At this point of the conversation it is important that you communicate your intentions. After you have had a brief relationship building conversation, it is important that you change the focus so you can discuss your objective, the business. You can go on to initiate this conversation by saying:

"....the reason I'm calling you is to ask if you had a chance to review the information I gave you?"

If the answer is 'no', you shouldn't be disappointed, but there is a fair chance your prospect isn't interested in what you have to offer. If they were not bothered to review the information in the time you gave them, there is a good chance they are not really interested in fixing their problems, so this is just another way of pre-qualifying your prospects. Additionally this question will help to determine how motivated they are. In our experience the best networkers are the ones that take a pro-active approach and are motivated right from the start.

A good tip to remember is that if you are not actively involved in solving your problems, there is a fair chance that the problem will never go away. Therefore unless your prospect offers a legitimate excuse, you are probably best to cross them off your list and explain to them that your opportunity only works for people who are self motivated and actively working towards achieving their dreams and that maybe in the future the opportunity might come at a better time. Having said this it is important that you remain friendly with your prospects at all times, even if your prospect has indicated that they aren't interested in your offer.

If their response is 'yes' they have reviewed your material, great your now ready to make the sale.

Step 2. What to say when your prospect has reviewed your business information

The key concept behind a successful follow up and you closing the deal is to get your prospect thinking about the positive aspects of your business opportunity. It is important to distinguish that by 'positive aspects' we mean those as they are perceived by your prospect, which are not necessarily the same positive aspects that you see.

Additional to this, one of the biggest tips we can give you is that the person asking the questions is the person in control of the conversation. Learning to ask the right questions can go a long way towards closing the deal and is an important skill to master in the prospecting process. By the right questions we mean those that will return a favourable response. When you put these two important concepts together you have a powerful formula for success. That is, by asking the right positively geared questions, you are both in control of the conversation and to some extent their response. Using this technique will assist you closing the deal as your prospects will essentially sell themselves.

By asking the right positively geared questions you are both in control of the conversation and to some extent their response. For example, if you were to ask:

— *"What did you think about....?"* This allows your prospect to discuss both the pros and cons and more often than not they will go on the defensive straight away. Therefore a better question to ask would be:

— *"What did you like about.....?"* This now limits your prospect to focus on the positives. The more positive your prospect is towards the information you offered them, the greater the chance of making a sale. This is a skill used and taught by the most successful salespeople in the world.

If they do respond on the negative and try to dismiss your offer straight away, try to regain control by re-asking the question?

"Ok, but was there anything you did like about what you saw?"

If they respond negatively again, accept that they are genuinely not interested and concede that with such a negative and narrow minded attitude you wouldn't want to be working with them anyway. Remember—professionals sort, amateurs convince—this is just another step in the qualifying process. Thank them for their honesty then change the conversation to finish on a positive note.

In a typical response to this question, most of your prospects will highlight the positive aspects of your business opportunity. Take note as these factors will become critical in your final sales pitch when closing the deal. Remember you want them to continue to focus on the positive, so try to get your prospect to elaborate on these positive aspects as much as possible. For example, if they respond by saying they "like the products", your goal is then to get them to go into more detail as to why they like the products. This deepens the pre-selling process as essentially they are convincing themselves as to why they should look into this further.

Once they have started to concede that there are a number of positive aspects to your opportunity, your next goal is to marry your solution with their goals.

"Do you see how (what they like about the business) could help you to (achieve their hot button)?

If they are going to have objections about your offer this is where they will normally come up. Remember - to be in control of the conversation you need to be the person asking the questions. If they don't have any objections, and they continue to speak positively about your opportunity great, skip ahead and go straight into your final sales pitch.

Objections

If your prospect gives an objection then you need to regain control of the conversation and get your prospect to reiterate their hot buttons. "I understand what you're saying and I know how important it is that you pay your children's tuition (or what ever your prospect hot buttons are). But imagine if a home business (or your opportunity) could help you to secure your children's education (or what ever your prospect hot buttons are), how would this make you feel?"

Straight away you're back on the positive. Another approach to consider is offering them a solution to their problem that appears out of reach or too hard for them and then to follow it with an easier/ ore favourable alternative.

The Final Sales Pitch

The final sales pitch should be a reinforcing statement that basically highlights that you can help this person to overcome their problems and provide the necessary support along the way. As stated above it might be something like:

"It's obvious that you are passionate about your dreams and you definitely appear to have the qualities that we're looking for. If you're willing to give achieving (their hot buttons) a serious go, I'd love to get you started and meet our team. So what do you say?"

At this point their response will either be favourable or not. Regardless it is important that you remain friendly with your prospect and never argue. Remember - professionals sort, amateurs convince.

We strongly encourage that you prospect in an ethical way. If you are prospecting a person who you believe is not suited to your opportunity or does not have the skills you believe are necessary to be a part of your team, you need to inform this prospect that you don't think that this opportunity is right for them. Your job is to find the right people, not just the willing. Do not recruit distributors just for the sake of building your downline, to do so will only provide short term gain and long term pain as you struggle with retention and a breakdown in relationships. Additionally this can negatively impact on the reputation of your company as well as the network marketing industry as a whole. Your goal is to find self-motivated individuals, who you believe, will actively work towards building a network marketing business and achieve their goals.

Whilst many network marketers are faced with this moral dilemma frequently, trust us when we say to take an ethical approach. Not only does it do the right thing by your prospect, your business, your company and the industry, you'd also be surprised how much more attractive your business will become once your prospects are aware that you only recruit the best.

❖❖❖

5

ENROLLING IN NETWORK MARKETING

The world of network marketing is undergoing a radical, positive transformation. The new wave of network marketing companies shatters the myths commonly associated with old-school direct sales. Even more interestingly, the social implications of these new companies are nothing less than groundbreaking.

In order to build a network marketing dynasty, there are essentially two critical areas upon which to focus. The first is massive and consistent action, persistently following up on all your prospects in a timely manner. The second is to create value and rich possibilities as you communicate to others the gift embodied by your income opportunity.

Massive action is best supported by a daily action commitment, namely a promise you make to yourself to speak with a certain minimum number of people each and every day. Initially your conversations will be predominantly prospecting conversations, introducing others to your company, products, and most importantly, to your income opportunity.

As you fill your pipeline with enough prospects, you'll want to add timely follow-up conversations to support your prospects in their evaluation of your opportunity. For some, it will be a fit. For others, it will not. Remember to always ask those who are not interested if they would be willing to support you by becoming a product customer. Also ask if they would suggest a few other individuals who might be open to evaluating your opportunity. When you ask, in this way, for three to five referral names, many of your prospects will be happy to oblige.

RULES OF ENROLMENT

Remember, your ultimate success depends not on how well you can make others do what you want them to do but on how effectively you can identify ways to contribute to their lives. With this in mind,

1. Give up your right to force anyone to do anything just because you want him or her to do it. Sales pressure, begging, and coercion are of little value in this business. You may get some to sign up just to get you off their backs, but if they are to build a business long-term, they must possess self-motivation. Beggars are also not very attractive as business partners, so you'll want to always maintain a posture that communicates: "I'd love to have you join our team but I am not attached to your doing so."
2. Look to contribute value to your prospects' lives. After hearing your presentation, do your prospects know that you are currently or will soon be successful in this business and if they join you, they will be as well? If you do your job correctly, your prospect should be thinking, "This must be lucky day!" After all, it is a true gift you are sharing with your prospects and it would be a privilege for any prospect to have someone as committed as you for a business partner and sponsor!

Let's look closer at some conversational goals upon which you might focus.

Create True Value

Enrollment success depends upon creating great value for your prospects. Is your intention to have your prospects realize that you are offering them some very exciting possibilities to explore? You may want to first check your own belief level. Is your belief rock solid and unshakable with regard to the network marketing concept? Are you proud of what you do or might you be ashamed to some degree of being affiliated with a marketing technique that many mistakenly confuse with a pyramid scheme? Are you totally sure that you will be successful and that you know exactly how to support others to be successful? If the answer to any of these questions is not resoundingly affirmative, your prospect is probably sensing that something is missing for you as well. You may be saying the right words but your energy may give away your uncertainty.

The best way to handle any lacking belief is to become convinced of the value of each aspect affecting your offering. Research the network marketing industry. Be able to distinguish the great companies possessing integrity and the ability to impact people's lives from the sleazy schemes that won't be around a few years from now. Be sure your company fits all the criteria of a company you can be proud to represent. Get to know your product line inside and out. Learn and experience the reasons it is extraordinary and worthy of your highest recommendation. Know that the income opportunity is totally sound. Speak with others who have achieved different degrees of financial freedom, thanks to your opportunity. When you are so sure that you made the right choice, you will convey that belief to others through the energy you put forth.

Discover What It Is Like in Your Prospect's World

FLOP them! Ask about their family, where they live, their occupations, and passions or hobbies. Be genuinely concerned about who they are and what makes them special. Offer a sincere acknowledgement if appropriate. Make a friend. When you take the time to build the bond before sharing your information, your prospects will be more likely to listen to what you have to say.

Identify What Is Important to Your Prospects

How can you hope to understand what would be of interest to your prospects if you have not taken the time to find out what matters most to them? Where is there pain in their lives? What's missing in terms of money, security, fun, fulfilment, or freedom? How might your opportunity address any missing element?

A good way to gain insight into what might matter most to your prospect is to ask, "If money were no object, how would your life be different from what it is today? Would you still continue to work where you are working now? Would you retire early or pursue a hobby or special interest? Would you buy a new car or house? Would you pay off any debt or buy any toys? Would you live where you currently do or move somewhere else? How would you be able to impact your family's lives differently? Would you travel or play more than you presently do? What would change as a result of the financial freedom you had created?" By getting your prospect to dream a bit, you will gain insight into the areas that would make this a game worth playing for them.

Develop a Bond Based on Mutuality and Look to Contribute to Them in Some Way

People like to work and associate with others who share things in common with them. The more areas of interest your prospect shares with you, the more likely he is to like you, trust you, and want to be with you.

If you also can identify some ways that your income opportunity might contribute to him or how your products might be a fit, you will be that much closer to developing yet another thing in common: your business.

With insight regarding some areas in which your offering could contribute to your prospect's life, you can now make a suggestion or request to support him in taking the next step in the evaluation process. Such a request must be in your prospect's best interest, not just in yours! He must be able to understand your motivation for making the request. He must trust that you have his best interests at heart, because you've taken the time to get to know what they are.

Let's now take a look at how we might weave the preceding conversational goals into our discussion to maximize our effectiveness in the enrollment process.

PROCESS FOR MAXIMIZING YOUR CONVERSATIONAL EFFECTIVENESS

Maximize your conversational effectiveness by paying attention to the following five steps:

Step 1: Create an opening to be heard. We create an opening to be heard by first listening to others. We do so as we build the rapport characteristic of the friendshipping process. As we make a friend, we establish an atmosphere of trust. We explore areas we have in common, thus building mutuality.

Perhaps the first step in getting a conversation off to a good start is to be respectful of the other person's time. Always ask if you are calling at a convenient time or if she would be better served to reschedule your conversation. Break the ice by first speaking about something you can identify about the person. Perhaps it is where she lives. You're from Maine and she's from California. Maybe you'll make a comment about how great it is today that technology allows people to be successful partners on opposite coasts. Comment on how you'd love to be able to have a reason to visit California, especially during those cold and snowy New England winters. It really doesn't matter what you talk about—just look for something to set a friendly, conversational tone that supports your prospect to feel at ease.

Step 2: Determine if your prospect is open to exploring if there may be a fit with what you do by getting permission to ask him a few questions. Do this before discussing your income opportunity with him. By asking permission, you lower the prospect's defenses as you ask those questions that will allow you to better understand his world.

A talkative prospect may take such an invitation to tell you all about his life story. You welcome this chance by asking follow-up questions and looking for areas of commonality while further developing rapport. For more reserved prospects, you may have to hone in on an easy opening question. You might say, "Where do you live now and have you always lived there?" As your prospect answers one easy question, it sets the stage for you to ask another. Loosen up the conversational mood as you build further rapport.

Step 3: Speak your commitment to your prospect in some way. You want your prospect to realize that she will not need to go it alone to become successful. In fact, you'll be there, by her side, to champion her every step of the way. By speaking your commitment to look without pressure or expectation on your part, you offer to explore if this would be something that would contribute to her life. Voicing your commitment to support her success by working hand-in-hand with her, while showing her exactly what it will take to be successful and then partnering with her in every way to make it happen, reinforces this pledge. This includes speaking to her prospects with her, training her and them, and coaching her team to achieve success. For many serious prospects, such a commitment should be a hard offer to turn down.

Step 4: Create rich possibilities that inspire action. As we have already discussed, it is our job to create value for our prospects. We will actually get paid in proportion to how well we accomplish this objective. When our prospects see a fit for the benefits we offer, believe they can accomplish their goals with our support, and are left with a positive expectation for their success, they will be inspired to get started and to take action.

Step 5: End by making a request that moves the conversation in a forward direction. Requests are the tools that enable us to direct a conversation to a powerful conclusion. You know the value of your company's offerings and what steps will best support your prospect to discover them. Most prospects will not know what to look for or where to get information to make an informed decision regarding whether your opportunity may have value for their lives. It's your responsibility to direct them to see the value. Do this by offering suggestions and making requests.

To increase the chance that your prospect will comply with your request consider the following key components to a powerful request:

– Your request must be in alignment with your prospects' needs, wants, and desires. It can't be just about you, to make you money, or to only serve your needs. Speak the reasons for your request to help your prospect understand why the action you are suggesting is in her best interests.

– Your request should have a timeline attached to it. Offer a choice of days for a next call. Ask if your prospect can watch a video by this Sunday night. When you put a time frame on your request, you ensure that it just doesn't hang out there indefinitely. Contrast this with a request to just "watch a video." Without specifying a "by when," you have no idea how long it may take your prospect to get around to it.

– Get confirmations from your prospect regarding your requests. With any request, your prospect has the option of either accepting or declining your request. He also may wish to let you know his answer at a later time. Or he may counter-offer with a reply that works better for him.

❖❖❖

6

TRAINING AND PERSONAL IMPROVEMENT

Network marketing training is almost like one of those vodoo subjects that people do not like to talk about. Isn't half of the allure in MLM the fact that anyone can do this? This is just a complete myth, the fact is that just like in any other business, you need proper training in order to be successfull. Here are three themes that you need to focus on when you are looking for great network marketing training.

First, the network marketing training should address who you should be marketing your MLM business, opportunity or product to. Still harassing your family and friends with your products, even though they don't want anything to do this it? Forget about that. Instead the MLM training should address something known as targeted marketing. At the core, targeted MLM marketing should teach you to focus your efforts on who actually is looking for what solution your product offers, or is looking for what your opporutnity can provide.

Second, your network marketing training should focus on exactly how to generate MLM leads. Now that you have the targeted marketing down, how do you convert those into leads? Using the advantages available in great internet network marketing training will help you alot. The way to go these days is to leverage online mediums and learn how to generate leads using things like pay-per-click advertising, social network marketing sites like Facebook, MySpace, and Twitter, along with some basic training on how the internet works.

Finally, the network marketing training should address how to convert those targeted MLM leads to either downlines or mlm product sales. Are you going to be calling all those leads personally? Will you be directing to a sign-up or purchase page? However you do it, that training absolutely needs to address these issues.

ACHIEVE SUCCESS WITH EFFECTIVE TRAINING

Let's look at what training structures you can put into place to facilitate their advancement.

Teleconference Opportunity and Training Calls

Many network marketing companies corporately sponsor daily or weekly opportunity and training calls. In those instances where there are no such company-supported calls, it would serve the organization's building efforts to have top leaders step up and host these conferences on a weekly, if not more frequent, basis. Often, scheduling an opportunity call early in the week that feeds new distributors into a "get started training call" a couple of days later works well. Some keys to such a system's success include:

- Communicating the importance to support the calls. Calls that are poorly attended communicate the wrong impression to new listeners that this company must not be growing!
- The calls need to be high energy and interactive. It often works best when at least two leaders partner to co-lead the call, bouncing thoughts off each other.

- To conduct a powerful opportunity call, the presenter could first share her personal story regarding when and how she was introduced to the company, products, and opportunity. Where her life was before her involvement with her network marketing company can be contrasted with where she is now in terms of happiness, fulfilment, fun, and finances. She can briefly speak about the vehicle to create wealth, namely (1)network marketing, (2) the stability and credibility of the company, (3) the unique qualities and value of the products, and (4) the exciting nature of the income opportunity. She can then ask for some product testimonials and then request some income testimonials.

  Those distributors who share their stories and testimonials should stress the life-changing nature of the opportunity. The call leader should thank all attendees, acknowledging those who generously shared their stories or offered testimonials. Lastly, the call should end with a call to action, encouraging prospects to get with the person who invited them to the call to further explore the possibilities and have all their questions answered.

- Training calls should follow along with the company's duplicate system. Subsequent calls might include a brief summary of the company's compensation plan: (1) going over each of the products in detail to outline their benefits and target markets, (2) setting up the new distributor's office, (3) designing an action plan, (4) creating a names list and supplementary lead sources, and (5) role-playing some typical prospecting conversations. The training call should stress the simplicity of the system. Using a prerecorded call to three-way in a prospect, offering a web site URL to visit, and suggesting a follow-up call with a success-line business partner are simple ways for even the most reluctant new team member to get started.

Local, Regional, and National Meetings

Your organization will grow most rapidly when you are able to take advantage of a strategy to funnel your prospects and distributors into local, regional, and national meetings. All company-approved meetings are promoted on all conference calls, in the monthly newsletter and bonus check flyers, on the corporate web site, and in all other communications to the field. Randy Anderson has built a dynasty utilizing this process of continually promoting the next impending event. Randy recommends the following strategies to make this structure work:

— Encourage local weekly meetings in all areas where a leader can take responsibility for hosting them and growing their attendance numbers. These meetings may be small at first, consisting of a local business builder who steps into leadership to invite a few guests or new distributors. As the local group grows in number, each distributor takes responsibility for inviting at least one new person to every weekly meeting. When the size of any particular weekly meeting reaches 15 or more, the group is encouraged to form a second local weekly gathering.

As long as distributors continue to bring prospects and new distributors to these functions, the agenda can consist of a brief 30-minute opportunity introduction to the company, products, and income opportunity followed by a training focusing on some basic element of getting started properly to build a successful business.

The entire weekly meeting should take no longer than two hours. It should be held on the same day and time and at the same place each week so as to avoid confusion. These meetings are best conducted in the comfortable confines of a home or office.

— The weekly meetings feed into the local monthly meetings. When these meetings are attended by at least 40 to 50 people, they can be hosted in a hotel or function facility meeting room. If they are smaller in size than that, it is best to conduct them in a home, office, or private restaurant room. It is important not to convey the impression that the business is not growing by holding poorly attended meetings in a formal, large meeting facility. The monthly meetings can start off with a brief opportunity presentation to support any prospects in attendance. All local leaders should share the room setup, agenda outline, and speaking assignments so as to edify everyone who has opted to step into a leadership role. The meeting should last between four and six hours and include lunch or dinner to add an element of fun and strengthen the relationships among attendees.

— The local monthly meetings serve to funnel people into larger regional meetings. These meetings typically are conducted in a hotel function facility. They last an entire day and end with a social and dinner event.

It is valuable for a top distributor or accomplished leader to close these events. The ability to come and listen to someone who is living the dream, thanks to the great opportunity made possible by your company, is an important factor in stimulating interest and driving attendance.

These meetings should focus on the steps to achieve success, with a goal of inspiring attendees to step into a massive action mode. They should also highlight success stories and recognize the accomplishment of distributors advancing in compensation plan positional rank and achieving organizational growth.

Distributors should leave these functions motivated to share in the success they witnessed others already realizing.

They should also be inspired to commit to attending the company's national functions. The national meetings are typically company supported and organized, though they may be conducted and headlined by top field leaders. These meetings are often held in fun family resort locations, giving the distributor's family a reason to join him or her and make the event a memorable vacation.

Because these meetings have the goals of conducting trainings to equip distributors with important success distinctions, acknowledge leaders achieving success, introduce new products and programmes, and most importantly to build relationships, partnerships and belief, it is best if meetings span the course of two or three days.

The intention of these events is to leave distributors with the knowledge of how to build a successful organization while inspiring their desire to go out and do whatever it takes to make this dream a reality. The most successful field leaders typically partner with the company's corporate team to make these events most powerful.

By creating such a structure with meetings at each level that feed other meetings, distributors are given the knowledge needed to build a successful business as well as a system to eventually transform new distributors into accomplished leaders. At each level, distributors are encouraged to stretch and step into a succession of leadership roles. Having such a structure also generates the excitement that comes from promoting the next impending event.

COMBINE TRAINING WITH MASSIVE ACTION

It is important to stress the extreme value of combining training with massive action. Doing so will avoid your new partner's thinking that she will need to know every aspect of your product line and business plan before she can step into action. The most successful training lessons result from feedback that you will offer your new partner as she prospects and brings new people to the team. Be sure to let your new partners know that they have your full permission to mess up and fall flat on their faces. In fact, this is the most effective way for them to learn as they gather the successful distinctions that come with building a business. Many new distributors will be reluctant to make a mistake, thinking that they might blow a chance to enroll a great prospect. To the contrary, there is no scarcity of prospects in the world. Competence and eventual mastery will result from trial and error and never-ending improvement as part of the learning process.

By giving your team members plenty of room to make mistakes, you'll be encouraging them to step into their personal power. This power is greatly enhanced by your nonattachment to anyone needing to get involved. The posture you'll want to communicate is that you'd love any particular person to join your team—but the choice is theirs. You'll do quite well either way. There's no desperation and no scarcity of interested people who would welcome the chance to work with you in partnership toward their success. This logically takes us to the topic of personal improvement.

PERSONAL DEVELOPMENT

Even the most experienced and seasoned network marketers can benefit from a programme that examines their personal strengths and weaknesses.

Create a Personal Development Structure for Supporting Your Success

You're in consistent and persistent massive prospecting action. You are honouring your commitment to speak with a minimum number of prospects daily while following up with all interested parties on a timely basis. Let's look at some personal development structures you might put into place to gather feedback regarding how you can maximize your personal effectiveness with everyone you speak.

Rate each prospecting communication you have (1 = ineffective, self-absorbed, no rapport developed to 10 = powerful, rich value created, you've bonded with your prospect) *with respect to how powerfully you guided the conversation.*

Many network marketing companies are blessed with competent coaches. Many also support personal development programmes to champion their distributors to be their very best. If you'd like to explore a programme to champion your productivity, success, and happiness, our company, the Center for Personal Reinvention, offers custom-tailored programmes for individuals and groups.

Grow Yourself along with Your Business

Using the following list as a memory jogger, identify the top five qualities of a successful leader and business partner *that would most impact your success.*

Qualities of an Effective Network Marketing Leader

— Authentic

— Disciplined
— Focused
— Believable
— Visionary
— Supportive
— Inspirational
— Does Not Take Rejection Personally
— Has Enthusiastic and Contagious Belief Level
— Interested in Personal Growth and Development
— Has High Level of Physical Energy
— Willing to Contribute to Others
— Has Integrity
— Can Make and Keep Commitments
— Compassionate
— Sensitive
— Organized
— At Peace
— Persistent
— Consistent
— Teachable
— Empowers Others
— Ambitious
— Committed
— Entrepreneurial
— Team Player
— Confident
— Powerful
— Vulnerable

— Willing to Sacrifice for the Future
— Able to Bond with Others
— Positive, Upbeat Attitude
— Burning Desire to Succeed
— Follows Up and Follows Through
— Positive Expectation
— Works in Partnership
— Interested in Others
— Doesn't Dump Information
— Proactive—Takes Initiative
— Good Communication Skills
— Positive Expectation
— Committed
— Good Self-Image
— Intuitive
— Empathetic
— Happy to Serve
— Genuinely Humble
— Good Listener

In reinventing yourself to maximize your effectiveness, what qualities will support your declaration as a leader? Ask your coaches and partners for feedback about what qualities they see would best support your effectiveness and productivity in each area.

Let's take a few moments to briefly define and discuss each quality or area in order to provide you with better insight regarding how each might apply to enhancing your productivity.

Authenticity is about how you come across to others. When what you say is in alignment with what you do and who you are, others perceive you as authentic. Authenticity comes from speaking in a conversational tone with an intention to communicate from your heart to the other person's heart. Contrast this with the opposite qualities of phoniness, hype, or falseness. Are you looking with your prospects to determine if your offering may be a fit or are you trying to sell him something he has no interest in considering? Might you resemble a sleazy salesperson trying to unload a broken-down, used car on a reluctant victim? Believability results from authentic communication and actions that display integrity. People who are believable avoid hype and exaggeration. They tell the truth responsibly, even when it becomes uncomfortable to do so. They follow through on the commitments they make and value their reputation over the convenience of saying or doing what's expedient at the moment.

Discipline is about treating your income opportunity as a serious business. If you find yourself often watching television or making excuses to get out of prospecting, you lack this trait. The best example of a disciplined business builder is one who consistently honours her daily action commitment—no matter what the distractions and circumstances. On those days when it is impossible to do so, she commits to making up for the lapse with additional calls. People with discipline choose to honour their commitments to their vision rather than to their comfort and convenience.

Focus implies keeping your eye on the prize. It means ignoring distractions and effectively handling interruptions so they do not interfere with your achievements. Having focus means returning yourself and your prospect to the topic at hand when it is obvious that you've strayed.

Visionaries see the big picture. They are not derailed by what they see as temporary challenges or interruptions en route to realizing their dreams. They inspire themselves and others to go after those things worth pursuing. They lead others to see possibilities in every situation rather than the limitations. They live out of a current, invigorating vision that empowers people by speaking what they are committed to achieving while challenging them to join in the quest.

Supportive leaders are team players. They create win-win scenarios wherever they go. They build relationships, empower others, and are champions of people and causes. In contrast, nonsupportive people are self-absorbed, with little interest in putting themselves in the other person's world. They fail to realize what their obstinacy is costing them in terms of generating possibilities and building relationships.

Inspirational people support others to see possibilities outside the box of usual familiarity. They are possibility thinkers, seeing ways to make things work where others do not. They are card-carrying visionaries who inspire others to join them in their visions and to create visions of their own.

Confident networkers know the value that their products and opportunity embody. They exude an attractiveness that causes others to want to join them and be in their presence. Confidence is born of belief in the gift they have to offer others. They share this gift with pride and positive expectation. Because of their confidence, they are self-motivated to stay in action, knowing for certain that their success is imminent.

Personal power results when one lives and acts in alignment with one's values. It, too, is a result of the confidence that comes from knowing one has the ability to impact the lives of others. People possessing personal power are charismatic and able to champion others to believe in themselves and achieve the type of success that results when actions are in alignment with vision. They are proactive and take initiative instead of waiting for things to fall into place by themselves. They realize there will always be challenges that allow those with a lesser commitment to make excuses and wait until the timing is just right to act. By taking responsibility for everything that shows up in their lives and in their businesses, these leaders realize that "if it's going to be, it's up to me!" They realize they are the source of whatever manifests around them and so they take it upon themselves to bring about the result they desire through bold actions.

Vulnerability does not imply weakness or failure. On the contrary, it's the ability to transparently convey who one really is on a personal or spiritual level. Vulnerability is the result of speaking and acting authentically. There is no need to hide, cover up, or pretend by wearing a mask. Others get who you really are because your actions are transparent. The most effective leaders possess a genuine humility that allows others to be comfortable in their presence. The opposites of vulnerability are callousness, arrogance, and defensiveness. One effective way to let others in and express vulnerability is to tell something about yourself that shows your humanity. Perhaps you might relay a story or share an incident that supports others to see the softer side you may ordinarily conceal from view. Ironically, many times, those individuals unafraid to share their vulnerability are perceived as inspirational and stronger because they do not hide their flaws. They, instead, use them to make others feel comfortable around them.

A willingness to sacrifice for the future is a quality essential to building a successful networking business. There will be many times when moving one's business forward will require a concerted effort in the present, regardless of whatever distractions may show up in life. Though it is wise to integrate life and business whenever possible, leaders, at times, will need to give their business priority over other distractions.

The ability to bond with others is a prerequisite for developing effective relationships and partnerships. Lone rangers do not make dynasty builders! There is simply no way to build a large, successful organization without empowering others to step into a leadership role. Empowerment comes from relationship-building and inspiring others to be their best. Supporting others to get to know you, like you, and trust you will strengthen the bonds that make for long-lasting relationships and business partnerships.

Leaders do not take rejection personally. They know that when prospects are not receptive to becoming involved in their opportunity, it has nothing to do with personal rejection. Perhaps the timing is not right for the prospect or they may not see themselves being successful in building a network marketing business. By not taking rejection personally, these leaders adopt an empowering interpretation that keeps them inspired to stay in massive action until such time as they identify enough other empowered, self-motivated leaders required to build their networking dynasty.

An enthusiastic and contagious belief level is the fire that spreads from those possessing this quality to those they prospect and those who join their team. Possessing this uplifting and charismatic positive expectation results from a surety that one is now, or soon will be, successful and so will those who join this person's organization. True belief comes across as an appealing and electrifying energy. It goes well beyond words alone to convey the genuine excitement that results from a certainty of achieving success. Those who are able to communicate this level of belief in the brightest possible future attract others with a magnetism that is lacking in those plagued by doubt and reservations.

An interest in personal growth and development separates those who make small, incremental advances from those who experience breakthrough performance levels. Those who commit to the process of constant and never-ending improvement in their lives and businesses are never content to stop learning and growing. They know that there is no arriving. The minute they forget this fact, they are back in the downward spiral that will kill their forward progress, damage their relationships, and remind them of their need to return to their commitment to perpetual growth and discovery. This quality separates the know-it-alls from those who view life as a continual process of self-discovery.

A high level of physical energy and a positive, upbeat attitude is important both from the standpoint of being able to sustain a busy schedule of prospecting, following up, training, and coaching as well as from the perspective of giving off an energy that is attractive to others. No one wants to partner with a person who appears ready to nod off to sleep at any minute. It is too easy to mistake low physical energy for lack of enthusiasm for what you do. An attractive energy level is upbeat but not frenetic. If you fear that your energy level may not be attractive to others, request feedback from your partners as you work on projecting a solid, empowering, and enthusiastic energy to everyone with whom you communicate.

A willingness to contribute to others and work in partnership is another attractive quality that will cause prospects to want to join us in partnership. People can smell a self-centered, me-first attitude a mile away. True leaders are happy to serve others. When our focus is on the success of others, we will be rewarded for our generosity of spirit tenfold. Prospects will clearly see our commitment to do whatever it takes to champion their success and will want to take advantage of this gift. The opposite quality of "what have you done for me lately?"

communicated in what we say and don't say will repel others, who will seek to distance themselves from such a selfish and self-serving attitude. Because success in network marketing demands a commitment to working effectively in partnership, those who shun this trait find themselves without support, making their task that much more difficult. As a result of a commitment to be a *team player,* we will be much more likely to attract other team players who model our example.

Having integrity and the ability to make and keep commitments are important prerequisites for building trust. Integrity is simply walking your talk. People with integrity can be counted on by others to come through on their promises. Those lacking integrity will not be held in high esteem as leaders. Their word will be questioned and their ability to do what they say they will do will be doubted. After displaying a regular pattern of failing to follow through on commitments, one loses credibility as others decide to stay away to avoid letdown.

Compassion is the result of getting into the other person's shoes and experiencing his challenges as if they were your own. People appreciate those who have compassion for their situations. Empathy or an appreciation for what another is going through is not the same as sympathy, which implies feeling bad for another whom we hold as incapable of dealing with the adversity presented. We can have compassion for the challenges of others without buying into their excuses or lack of commitment.

Possessing sensitivity allows us to be aware of the difficulties inherent in a situation. Those lacking sensitivity are wrapped up in their own world, often at the expense of others. This negative quality repels others who see insensitive people as cold, aloof, or unfeeling. Others will be more likely to want to work in partnership with those who possess the sensitivity of appreciating the challenges and limitations of others.

Organized people are typically productive people. Those lacking organizational skills frequently drop the ball and let others down because they are unable to effectively manage and honour their commitments. Organizational skills are necessary to make the most effective use of time. Often, those lacking these skills simply require a support structure to assist them in their ability to lend order to their lives and businesses. Such structures may include adding a PalmPilot, day planner, contact software, filing system, or other reminder or organizational system to set priorities and add a degree of order to replace chaos. Becoming organized means gaining clarity about your priorities and taking responsibility for recording them, classifying them, and honouring them.

Being at peace conveys energy conducive to having others want to be around you. On the contrary, nervousness, worry, fear, sadness, and anger repel others. Leaders who project this positive and attractive energy possess a positive self-image. Their high self-esteem supports them in handling rejection and not taking things personally while attributing positive interpretations to things that people say and do that allow them to remain upbeat and empowered rather than reactive and easily discouraged. Those who are at peace know that there are always valuable lessons to be learned at all times and with all matters. By trusting that things work out for the best and knowing that there is wisdom behind all worldly happenings, it serves us to trust that we will be fine in the end and can go about our days with the peace and serenity that come from this knowledge.

Consistency in network marketing refers to regularly repeated actions that will support a desired result. The best example of a consistent action plan is a daily action commitment, namely a pledge to engage in a minimum number of conversations on a daily basis. Persistency implies tenacious follow-up. It is such a commitment to follow-up and follow through that will produce the greatest returns. Consistency without persistency —will not produce the maximum number of enrollments possible. You will find that some of your most productive leaders will result from the persistency of a fourth, fifth, or sixth contact attempt.

Being teachable and coachable is a necessary element of duplication, and duplication is necessary for the maximum growth of an organization. Teachable team members are open to learning about and implementing processes that work. Coach-ability refers to an openness to listen to and consider feedback to explore ways to be more effective with people and more productive in growing the business.

Being interested in others and aware of the need to empower them is an essential component for building leaders. We must be sincerely interested in their well-being, while willing to commit to their success, not just our own. When we seek to manipulate or control others, we make them small and dependent upon us for their confidence and power. Since our income in network marketing is usually proportional to the number of leaders we empower to step into a leadership role of their own, failure to make others great will dramatically impact our bottom line.

An ambitious and burning desire to succeed together with an entrepreneurial nature will support people to do whatever is necessary to build a huge networking business. However, be aware that desire alone without a positive expectation to succeed will not be sufficient to manifest success. Desire alone represents the wanting of something that is currently missing or not yet attained. Look at how many people *want* to be rich and happy but are poor and miserable, instead! Consider how many overweight people *want* to be thin. Wanting or desiring alone, without a positive expectation focuses on the absence of what is desired rather than on the belief in its ultimate manifestation. So to be most empowering, combine a burning desire with an unshakable belief in the end result you seek.

Commitment to achieving a result is certainly one of the most critical qualities essential for success in network marketing. We are all committed to something. But that something is often our comfort or convenience, rather than doing whatever it takes to generate a desired result.

It may mean lying or stepping over the truth instead of doing the right thing and speaking our truth responsibly. In contrast, the right-hand path represents the path of heart, the road to our dreams' fulfilment. Moment by moment, we have the ability to recognize our chance to choose and decide deliberately to follow the path that will support our goals and vision, instead of our comfort. As a key part of your personal development plan, pay attention to the many opportunities you have daily to select the path of heart rather than the path of convenience. You will successfully develop this skill by continually recognizing your ability to choose and then acting in alignment with your commitments.

Being a good listener with good communication skills is critical to leaving our prospects with a sense that they have been heard and honoured. Being a good listener means both asking insightful questions and then quietly listening to what the person has to say without interrupting. Successful networkers listen to what others say, and, just as importantly, listen to what they do not say. They are highly *intuitive.* Often, by reading between the lines and paying attention to the unspoken communication, we can derive our greatest insights into where our prospects are in the discussion. We are always listening to something. However, too often that something is the frenetic chatter going on in our own brains, instead of what our prospects are really saying. To be a good listener, all it takes is to recognize when you are not listening and simply to return yourself to your commitment to listen attentively. Good listeners *do* not simply dump information upon their prospects. They do not talk at others but speak to them, ever mindful of not cutting them off or of stepping over their concerns, questions, and statements.

To create your own personal development structure to support your business success, start by selecting your top 5 to 10 areas upon which to focus. Use the same structures we previously discussed to gauge your improvement on a daily basis. Decide to work on one quality at a time, starting with those traits you believe would make the greatest impact on your business if you were to master them. After each conversation you have, rate yourself with respect to how well you manifested that particular quality. Ask yourself, "How can I enhance my next conversation by addressing this area?" Look also at those skills where you are not yet proficient. Declare yourself a novice in these areas and decide to work toward the goal of eventually developing mastery in each area. Always ask yourself, "What may be missing, that if put into place, would enhance this trait or area of development?" Success in taking on the positive traits you discover to be missing is as simple as recognizing when the particular qualities are absent and taking bold action to focus on putting them into place.

Ability to Generate Positive Interpretations

Success in network marketing is often due to how well

we respond to the rejection and other daily challenges that assault our belief level and threaten to throw us off track. It's rarely the actual words or situation that throws us into a tailspin. Rather, it's how we react to these words and events. The way in which we interpret another's statements and the meanings we attribute to those problematic situations present for us the real challenge.

Recognize! The key to maximizing your personal power often begins with your ability to recognize the opportunity to stop for a moment, evaluate your possible responses to any situation, and then act in a manner that reflects your personal power and effectiveness. This is often different from the way you would usually respond to such an occurrence in the heat of the moment. Your power begins by first recognizing your ability to *not react* to a stimulus but instead to deliberately respond in a manner that supports you. Reacting usually is the sort of behaviour consistent with a mood of anger, fear, or sadness. The mood is your red flag to stop and to recognize that you now have an opportunity to step into your power. According to Mike Smith of Bridgequest, anger is most people's predominant mood. If this is true for you, you will be well served to recognize when your anger flares up! It will be your cue to take the next step, which is to release the emotion. If you are one of those individuals who go quickly to the emotion of fear, recognizing this emotional flag will give you a warning sign to catch yourself in the act of being afraid. Similarly, if your predominant emotional reaction to stressful events is sadness, this emotion will signal your opportunity to choose your next actions wisely.

Release! Once you've identified your opportunity to notice your reactive emotion of anger, fear, or sadness, you can decide to deliberately release this emotion and the accompanying interpretation that has brought it about. Again, it's usually not the exact words that someone says or the action that takes place that brings about your anger, sadness, or fear. It's instead the meaning that you attribute to these words or actions. You make up interpretations that make you angry, sad, or afraid. For example, in speaking with your prospect, he may say, "Is this one of those pyramid schemes?" For some, this question will evoke anger. You may think, "How dare he accuse me of being involved with an illegal, sleazy pyramid scheme!" For others, it may generate fear. You may think, "Does he know something I do not? Can I get into trouble?" For others still, this question might bring about the emotion of sadness. "Here's yet another person who's finding a reason to reject me!"

Let's analyze what happened a bit closer. Mr. Prospect simply asked a question. Perhaps he was involved in a pyramid scheme at one time and lost money or got into trouble with the law. Perhaps he was testing our knowledge of our opportunity. Maybe he was looking for a way to make some fast money and was excited about this possibility. Maybe he was afraid you were going to ask him to spend money, and he was looking for an excuse to give him a way out. You simply do not know his motivation. So do not make something up that causes you to be angry, sad, or afraid! Release the mood you feel coming on along with the interpretation you created that resulted in the generation of your mood.

Reinterpret. Since we can't possibly know exactly what your prospect meant by his question, let's give him the benefit of the doubt and reinterpret it in such a way that allows us to further explore it, while remaining mood-free. We might take the interpretation that the prospect is interested in getting involved and is simply asking questions to establish the company's legitimacy. We might further interpret that he is providing us with an opportunity to listen to his concern and to educate him about the sterling reputation of your company and opportunity. We might see his question as a legitimate fear that he wants to resolve so he can move forward to the next level. Since we do not know what it's like in his world, we can't possibly know the true source of his question. So let's reinterpret it in a way that allows us to retain our power by gaining clarity about what his inquiry is all about. We might define his objection and say something like, "Tell me a bit more about your concern. Have you had a bad experience before with a pyramid scheme?" Or we might embellish his objection and say, "That's a great question! I also was concerned about the legitimacy of the opportunity when it was first presented to me. After all, there really are so many sleazy schemes out there! The last thing I'd want to get involved with is a company that is lacking integrity even the slightest bit." By not reacting emotionally, you can now maximize your ability to address your prospect's concern without the baggage of responding from a state of anger, fear, or sadness.

You will have ample opportunities in your network marketing business and in your daily life to recognize the opportunity to release an emotion that does not serve your personal power. Reinterpret your situation in such a way that you are personally empowered to respond in a manner that best serves your happiness, productivity, and effectiveness in communication. As you go about your day, notice when you become angry, sad, or afraid. Separate the facts regarding what was said or done from what meaning you attributed to these words or deeds. Create a new interpretation that has no negative emotions attached to it. This new meaning will keep you in relationship with the other person by giving her the benefit of the doubt. Your commitment to recognize the opportunity to respond to situations without the emotional baggage that diminishes your personal power will support effective communication and success in your business and relationships.

CONVERSATIONS FOR SUCCESS

The world we live and work in is marked by unprecedented change and fraught with new and complex challenges. For many of us, our network marketing businesses and our lives begin to look like an uphill struggle to survive instead of a fun and exciting opportunity to grow, risk, and play full out in partnership with others. The stresses, conflicts, and frustrations we experience daily need not be so. There exists another possibility:

- To live and work in choice, empowered by the challenges of life.
- To champion others to achieve excellence in a nurturing environment that fosters partnerships.
- To acquire the success principles that support mutuality, creativity, and harmony.
- To take on the art of listening and communicating in such a way that others are impacted to see new possibilities for accomplishment, partnership, and excellence.

Reinventing ourselves, our relationships, and our perceptions are the results of a never-ending commitment to our own personal magnificence and to that of others. It is made possible through the acquisition of approximately 50 key principles that cause people to begin to view life and people in an entirely different way. When people really *get* these principles, their lives, relationships, and new possibilities for breakthroughs show up from a totally fresh perspective.

7

STEPPING INTO LEADERSHIP

The network marketing industry has provided more millionaires in the last ten years than in any other industry. Network marketing is all about leadership. Leadership is the ability to influence and inspire others to follow you.

Stepping into a leadership role always begins with a decision to do so. No matter what evidence we may have accumulated to convince ourselves to the contrary, we all possess the power to be transformed into self-declared, empowered leaders whenever we decide to take the leap. How do you take this leap? The same way you jump off a mountain. You just do it!

For a leader, the decision to lead is always followed by a declaration. We each possess the personal power to declare our new commitment to leadership. The decision to lead is never contingent upon our past. Most of us can prepare a pretty strong case backed by all sorts of disempowering evidence to support that we are *not* leaders. By boldly declaring our new commitment to lead, we now get to determine exactly what leadership will look like for us. We can take responsibility for formulating a clear and compelling vision of how our leadership will manifest into the world. We also get to envision the results of this leadership and the effect it will have on the lives of others and on the world at large.

Leadership means that we are committed to powerfully acting in alignment with our commitments and vision. Contrary to our cultural paradigm, leaders often do not have all the answers. Many times, they simply need to risk and act from their values, in line with the results they desire to manifest. As self-appointed leaders, we can ask ourselves, moment-by-moment, "What would a leader do in this situation?" By asking this question, we decide to act in a manner congruent with how we see ourselves—as leaders!

In our network marketing businesses, we can apply these principles to step into leadership whenever we choose. No evidence is required to support this decision. Our decision to lead is not based upon volume or company position. Our decision to step into leadership results simply from a courageous commitment to act as a leader on a continual basis.

ELEMENTS OF NETWORK MARKETING LEADERSHIP

As network marketing leaders, let's examine some components critical to effective leadership.

1. At the foundation of any decision to lead lies a clear and compelling vision. Your vision as a successful network marketing leader will encompass every aspect of your life and business. It will include a clear and motivating representation of the person you have decided to be. It will honour your most important values and reflect the manifestation of your life purpose as you share your unique gifts with the world. When you live your vision, your days will be spent in choice. As a result, you will manifest those things into reality that results from accomplishing the ideals most

important to you. Your vision will serve to motivate you to overcome all challenges and to do what's necessary to achieve the success you desire. Powerful visions are most effective when spoken at every opportunity. By speaking your vision, you will inspire others to want to join you in its accomplishment. You will also inspire many to create visions of their own, moved by your example. Your life will become an example of how a positive expectation can empower others to achieve breakthrough results in their network marketing businesses and in their lives.

As a network marketing leader, you will become proficient in showing people how to think *outside the box* to manifest great possibilities in their lives. As you incorporate vision work into your basic training, you will be sharing a gift that has the ability to empower and transform lives marked by resignation and suffering. You will inspire others to pursue their dreams with a newfound hope and expectation of success. More importantly, by teaching others to teach others to design lives that work optimally, you'll be duplicating the gift of empowerment and contributing the tools that can form a successful foundation of accomplishment and leadership.

2. Leaders execute bold action plans that move their lives and businesses in a forward manner. Visions without actions are not really visions after all; they are wishful hopes void of the power of commitment and positive expectation. Leaders take responsibility for manifesting their visions by formulating specific, detailed, and grounded action plans that will bring them about. They continually evaluate whether their actions are sufficient in quantity and effective enough in quality to

make their visions come true. Network marketing leaders are well-served to evaluate the efficacy of their actions on a weekly basis and make the adjustments necessary to realize their goals. They know that in order to inspire others and gen erate a result, their actions must be consistent over time and persistent in frequency. Successful networking leaders know their enrollment ratios—how many prospects they will need to speak with, on average, in order to identify and develop an on-fire, do-whatever-it-takes leader. They execute a long-term action commitment to speak with a minimum number of prospects about their business every day so that, based upon their success-ratios, they will bring about the number of new leaders necessary to build a business dynasty.

3. Leaders possess an unshakable belief in their ultimate success and in the success of those who join them in partnership to follow a grounded, detailed action plan. This belief comes across to others as infectious, enthusiastic, and inevitable. True leaders possess the ability to inspire this cer tainty of future accomplishment to their prospects and team members. They know and teach their partners that a positive expectation of success in building their network marketing dynasties will generate sufficient self-motivation to manifest this goal into reality. They also know that the opposite is also true: When one expects to fail, this expectation generates self-sabotage and resignation, eventually resulting in quitting and an interpretation of failure. Either way, belief produces a self-fulfiling prophecy. Because of this knowledge, by virtue of their actions, leaders instill belief in the network marketing concept, their company, products, income opportunity, and in

their own leadership abilities and those of their partners.

4. The most effective network marketing leaders display a transparent authenticity and attitude of service that endears them to those who partner with them. Leaders walk their talk by demonstrating that their actions are consistent with their promises. They build trust and credibility as they prove they can be counted upon by demonstrating their commitment time and again to the success of their partners. Effective network marketing leaders avoid hype, arrogance, and domination. They, instead, choose sincerity, genuine humility, and a commitment to champion and serve others. They know that projecting a false façade diminishes their personal effectiveness and ability to manifest their intended results on an organizational basis. They work on effectively listening to others, always looking for ways to better impact their ability to achieve success and realize their dreams.

   Leadership Exercise: How does your own leadership style limit your personal effectiveness? What qualities will you seek to develop to enhance your ability to impact others?

5. Successful network marketing leaders duplicate themselves by empowering others to step into a leadership role at every opportunity. They make others great, never small through manipulation or condescension. They do this through making powerful requests that have others see new possibilities that they may not have previously seen for themselves, always stretching them to grow outside their comfort zones.

Effective leaders become proficient at the art of acknowledgement, always on the lookout to catch others doing something right. They realize that their own success depends upon their ability to champion up-and-coming partners to become even more effective and impactful leaders than they were. They know that there is no shortage of opportunities to build leadership. They are ever vigilant for ways to take a step aside, out of the limelight, in order to support another person to shine and gain recognition.

PRACTICAL STEPS TO TAKING ON A LEADERSHIP ROLE

Now that you have declared yourself to be a network marketing leader, it's time to seek out every possible opportunity to stretch who you are and step into your leadership role. Here are a few ways you might begin.

1. Be the source of leadership events in your local area. Commit to holding regularly scheduled weekly meetings at your home or office. If you do not have a home or office environment that lends itself to professional meetings, schedule them in a quiet room in a coffee shop or restaurant. It's important that you hold the meetings regularly, no matter how poor the attendance at first. The fact that others will see you as the local leader, taking responsibility for making these meetings happen, will help to establish your local leadership role. In the beginning, you might be the only person prospecting in your area and inviting others to attend your weekly function. As word gets out about your weekly meetings, more and more people will eventually attend and the numbers will build. There will come a day when it will grow to the extent that your meeting will be best supported to break up into a second and then a third local meeting. This will provide you with an opportunity to champion your own leaders to claim their

personal power and adopt this leadership role themselves.

2. Volunteer to speak in front of the room at your local monthly and regional meetings. Perhaps you will take on a particular product presentation or speak about some aspect of your company's compensation plan. You may start your public speaking career with a brief 5- to 15-minute segment on a topic you feel confident about addressing. Perhaps you might volunteer to be part of a panel, with each panel member speaking about a specific product or aspect of business building. This is a great way to learn to field audience questions in a format that allows support from others in case you require assistance with some of the more difficult questions. No matter what your confidence level, commit to taking baby steps to support your public speaking confidence and ability to entertain, educate, and impact a crowd. Become involved with your local Toastmasters organization to practice your public speaking skills on a friendly, supportive crowd. You might even interest a number of your fellow Toastmasters in your income opportunity!
3. Commit to host and lead a weekly opportunity or training call to introduce and support others in your growing organization or partner with other leaders cross-line by opening up the call to your entire company. By becoming the force for others to get together on a weekly call, you will be contributing to the growth of your own organization and those of others whom you will be inspiring with your leadership.
4. Setup an accountability circle with three or four other distributors. These can be leaders in your

own organization or cross-line in your company. Commit to reporting your actions to the other members of this "hot team" daily via e-mail or weekly with a group conference call.

RULES OF LEADERSHIP IN NETWORK MARKETING

Below are ten rules of leadership in network marketing. Work on incorporating them into your daily routine. A true leader takes consistent action, so it is important that you be consistent in your application of rules given below.

1. The Leader should have a goal larger than those that he/she leads. Your downline needs to know that you are planning for the future and also understand that your financial goals coincide with theirs.
2. The Leader must have an attitude greater then those that he/she leads. A leader is optimistic and focuses on the solutions and not the problems.
3. The Leader is responsible and admits when he/she has made a mistake. As a leader you are responsible for the things that go wrong in your team.
4. The Leader should make decisive decisions. All decisions are not correct, but if they are made with the right reasons in mind, then the right decisions will come more often. Strive to do the right thing and do not worry about doing things right.
5. The Leader always puts those that he/she leads first. When your downline sees that you are looking out for their best interests, they will work harder since they will realize that your goal is their success. People honestly don't care what you know until they know how much you care!

6. The Leader is in the front of the pack by setting an example to those that he/she leads. A good leader does not just tell others what to do but shows his team how to do it. Take the lead by setting the right example for your downline.
7. The Leader show's a commitment to integrity and character. Your downline will have confidence in you as a leader when they see you doing "the right thing".
8. The Leader strives for excellence in everything. Your attitude, appearance, work ethics, and dedication to excellence can help determine your success.
9. The Leader is determined to improving personal growth and development. The only way that you can be a leader that people will follow is to grow personally by learning the skills that are necessary to becoming a master network marketer.
10. The Leader display's a high level of persistence and determination. Genuine success takes time to achieve. How much time? As long as it takes!

These ten rules are important to any successful network marketing business. Develop your skill with people by following these rules and you will become a great leader. Ignore them, and some day you may wonder what happened.

WHAT DOES GOOD LEADERSHIP DEPEND ON?

These are critical for allowing you to get your ideas and thoughts across to your downline. If your downline has no idea what to do or how to do it, then how will they succeed or help you build your business?

Providing the proper motivation is another key area of successful leadership. Your downline will stagnate when not properly motivated. To increase motivation try challenging your downline with goals that may be out of the ordinary for them.

Teamwork. This means not only teaching your downline to work together but also for you to become part of the team. To become a better leader find out what your downline can do and recognize that they may have skills that could benefit your team.

Training and Education. Take the time to learn everything you can about your network marketing business. Contact your upline for help and advice.

8

MISCONCEPTIONS OF NETWORK MARKETING

Network marketing can be a pretty controversial subject. There are lots of people who love network marketing, then there are those that have heard of it but have misconceptions about it for various reasons. It is understandable because there is lot of misinformation out there and also people who give network marketing a bad name.

Network marketing is very unique in that it's the only business opportunity that's ever been marketed to the general public on such a massive scale. There's a horrible mess of hype, hot air, misconceptions, falsehoods, delusions, distortions, myths and downright lies that get passed along from one sponsor to the next. This is what happens when you take a bunch of people who don't have a clue about sales and marketing and have them tell a bunch of other people who don't have a clue about sales or marketing, to go make a bunch of money doing it.

The few techniques that actually do have some grounding in basic sales philosophy are all outdated and completely ineffective. They might work okay for you – if the year was 1984 – but in today's modern society, these kind of neanderthal tactics will get you slaughtered.

Using the wrong techniques – like trying to force a square peg into a round hole – makes it hard.

1. NOT EVERYONE IS YOUR PROSPECT

One of the most important lessons I've ever learned in marketing is this:

> People Who Try To Be Everything To Everybody, Wind Up Meaning Nothing Special To Anyone.

See, not everyone is looking to run their own business. Contrary to what we've been told, there are actually a substantial amount of people who are 100% content with being an employee and have no desire whatsoever to change that.

Some people love their job and wouldn't give it up for a million bucks. Some people despise network marketing and would rather be buried alive than be associated with it. Some people despise business in general. Some people think making lots of money is a bad thing. Some people don't have the funds to properly run a business. Some people are absolutely scared to death of anything that involves risk. Some people have plenty of money and aren't looking for anything else. Some people just plain old don't care. Some people don't have time. Some people just aren't cut out to be entrepreneurs and are better off working at McDonald's. Some people are perfectly content with where they are at in life and have no desire to change. That's fine.

Whatever the case, you do not need to convince anyone to get into this business. It's a waste of your time and energy to try and do so.

Who Finds Who First is Very Important

When you go head hunting and chase your prospect, the whole operation is doomed to failure because you're viewed as a nuisance! When they find you and seek you out, you're viewed as an expert.

Positioning makes all the difference in the world.

2. THIS REALLY ISN'T SALES

"It's not selling. It's sharing!" Doesn't that just give you warm fuzzies inside? This untruth also has a distant cousin which often takes the form of Gibberish like this:

> "Your family and friends should buy from you just because you're you. I mean, why would they give their business to some large corporation when they could give it to a close friend or relative. It's called keeping your money in close circles. People a hundred years ago used to do it."

Here are the two major side effects of this lie:

1. There's a huge deficiency of proper sales training because if it's not sales, then there's no need for sales skills. As a result, people are thrown to the wolves totally unprepared to retail their products and their opportunity.
2. People are set up for failure because they're given false expectations about how easy this is going to be. Labelling this whole business as "sharing" makes it sound like child's play. New distributors are given the impression they're doing one thing, when in fact it's something else entirely. They think this is going to be a cakewalk and when they find out it's not they aren't too likely to stick around.

When people are fed the idea that it's simply a matter of sharing, they're in for a very harsh reality check.

They go out and eagerly "share" their incredible product with all their family members, only to be sorely disappointed when they're shot down. Then they're baffled as to why it didn't work for them.

One of the main reasons people tell this lie is because they don't want to scare new prospects away.

They want people to get this nice, cozy feeling that all we're doing is telling the rest of the world about our wonderful product and people will be so swept away by our enthusiasm that they'll automatically buy.

After all, it's common knowledge that most people hate sales. So uplines and sponsors will beat around the bush and basically sugar-coat this inconvenient and uncomfortable fact:

If You Are In Network Marketing, You Are In Sales.

Understand this: Anytime you're asking another person to give you money in exchange for something, you're talking about sales.

Selling is Not Sharing and Sharing is Not Selling

We've all heard it before. Word of mouth is the most powerful form of advertising there is, right? Right.

What do you do when you see an incredible movie at the theatre? You tell your friends how awesome it was...how gripping the plot was...how engaging the actors were...blah, blah, blah, all that good stuff...and that they absolutely have to go see it. Same with eating out at a great restaurant or picking up your favourite artist's new CD.

People will be very likely to go spend money on these things after hearing a glowing report from you, their trusted friend.

Here's where the stick gets thrown into the spokes.

Your personal recommendation for all that stuff is so powerful because you have nothing to gain by "selling" them to your friends. As soon as you throw a financial interest into the mix, everything changes.

Both for you and for them.

For starters, you're not as comfortable. You don't feel as natural as you did with something you don't make money off of. Now you're forcing it and as a result, it just doesn't "flow" the same.

It's also different for them because they know you're making money from the deal. It's no longer an unbiased, "third party" opinion. People can smell an "incentivized" referral from a mile away. The whole dynamics of it has changed.

So the fact is, in network marketing you have now crossed over from the world of personal recommendation to the realm of direct sales. Don't let anyone tell you they're the same, because they're not.

Once you get this you'll understand that you do indeed need to learn effective sales skills. It isn't enough to just "recommend" your products to people you know.

Just because someone is your friend does not constitute a good enough reason for rhem to buy from you.

It's their hard earned money we're talking about here. And now you need to give them real, solid and compelling reasons to buy your product instead of all the similar ones out there.

Learning effective sales techniques is mandatory for success. You have to understand the sales process and what *really* motivates people.

3. ANYONE CAN DO THIS

This one is actually sort of a half-truth. A very dangerous half-truth. It can be very misleading because the simply fact of the matter is: *Not all network marketers are created equal.*

Everyone comes into this game with different advantages and disadvantages.

Some people have an enormous head start on others in terms of skills, time and money, and just because they were able to build an enormously profitable business in 24 months does not guarantee the next person will be able to.

The problem with statements like *"Anyone can do this business!"* is they imply that everyone—regardless of what their current situation is—can jump right in cold turkey and get the same results the heavy hitters got, just as fast.

Here's an example that's not uncommon.

Aruna, who holds a high paying executive position in the corporate world, decides to enter network marketing. Say she was the Vice President of Sales and Marketing for XYZ Corporation in Gurgaon, Haryana.

She's obviously got quite a background in sales or she wouldn't have that job. So right off the bat, she's way ahead of the pack. She's also already making a high six figure income as it is, which means two things:

First, she isn't dealing with the same kind of financial "crunch" and emotional stress that most people experience as they try to pay their monthly residual bills. And...

Second, she has plenty of cash to fund her new business venture.

Now, if you're looking at it from a "warm" market approach she also has truckloads of professional contacts to work with and these people have a lot of respect for her. Safe to say that pretty much everyone Jane knows is going to take her at least somewhat seriously if she brings a new idea to them.

She also has lots of professional sales contacts like herself, who also have tons of other professional sales contacts.

Do you think that someone who's a stay at home mom, secretary, college student, electrician, school teacher or bank teller is going to be able to see the same kind of results that Jane will in the same period of time? Probably not.

That's just one example – more of an old school one – but here's something else that happens all the time in mlm: When an upline with a big organization moves from one company to another and takes their whole team with them.

People on the outside looking in only see the rapid growth and big bonuses, but what they don't see is everything that's gone on behind the scenes. They're not getting the whole story. Yes, that upline brought in a huge team with them and began earning big money pretty much right away...but...it took years and years before they got to the point where they were actually in a position to do that.

They had to develop relationships and build a team that was loyal enough to them that they would even be willing to move with them wherever they went.

The point though is that...

> Everyone's On A Different Timeline And There Are Multiple Puzzle Pieces That Come Into Play That Determine How Quickly And How Easily A Person Will Make Money.

A big one is skill level.

Multi-level marketing is a sales business and the amount of sales skills that someone brings to the table in the beginning will have a huge impact on their success.

Anyone who wants to can develop sales skills. Some will take longer than others. Obviously someone who has 14 years of sales experience has a bit of an edge on someone with zero sales background and rather poor communication skills in general.

As far as money goes, every company is different when it comes to the initial start up costs. But aside from that, you do need an ongoing monthly marketing budget. Your upline or corporate team won't tell you this, but it's absolutely mandatory for running your business at full potential.

Without a marketing budget, you won't have the constant flow of fresh, qualified prospects you need.

There are two ways to get these leads for your business.

You can generate them through your own advertising or you can buy them from people who do that for you. You want to strive to generate your own because the advantages of doing so are enormous, but that's not to say buying leads from other sources doesn't have its place. Sometimes a combination of both approaches can be highly effective.

But either way, without leads, you don't have a business. Yes, you can start a network marketing business with very little time, money and skills. But what you start off with in the beginning will have a direct impact on how easy/difficult it will be for you and how long it takes you.

4. WE'LL BUILD YOUR BUSINESS FOR YOU

We've all seen the stuff on the net about fully automated online recruiting systems and how you can make outrageous money while they do all the work for you. Maybe you've tried a few. It certainly is an appealing idea. Who wouldn't want a turnkey system that does everything for them?

Well, here's the scoop on these type of deals: Why they appeal to people (not that that's hard to figure out)...what they can't do for you...and what a real automated system will do for you.

Network marketing is unique in that it's a business venture that's made available and offered to an extremely large amount of people. Never before has owning your own business had such widespread appeal.

With network marketing, the average person now has viable and realistic dreams of "making it big." 50 years ago, the road to riches was not so accessible. You had to start your own brick and mortar business with employees and all the works.

Here's where the problem comes into play.

You're a salesperson. All business owners are.

There's two things that every network marketer sells. One is the products that the company provides, such as telecommunications services, nutritional products, etc. etc.

But what makes you unique is that what you're also selling people is a business model. You're selling them a vehicle to achieve whatever financial goals they may have. It's really the first time that a business model has been sold to the public in this manner.

Thing is, the average person, who's known the employee model their whole life, doesn't know a lot about business. They don't understand basic business principles.

As a "customer," the average American is not business-savvy and does not know what to look for when selecting a home based business.

So to our instant-gratification-society, the idea of a "hands-off" system that will generate a ridiculous income with no investment of time or effort and just a little bit of money, seems like an actual possibility.

Business 101 is that somewhere along the line, a product or service must be sold to an end consumer. If a company says that "no selling is required on your part," this is a dead give away they're playing you for an idiot and you're about to be taken to the cleaners.

Just ask yourself this one simple and obvious question: *If no selling or anything else is required on your part, rhen why would they need you*?

The answer is: They wouldn't. If you're not contributing anything to the business besides a measly sign up fee, there would be no reason to pay you obscene amounts of money.

You have to be contributing something in order to justify getting paid. That's a fundamental economic truth. There's no such thing as something for nothing. There's no such thing as getting filthy rich with a Rs 4000 investment and no time or elbow grease.

Here's what you are contributing in a real legitimate mlm business to make it work: The indispensable human interaction.

This is why genuine network marketing companies do indeed need you and are willing to pay you big bucks for building a huge organization.

The key thing to understand is that *automated marketing systems are crucial to a successful business–but they can't do everything for you*

The truth is, an automated system is only half the equation. You, a real live human being, are the other half. No matter what anyone says, network marketing is and always will be built on relationships. As any stable, long-term business is.

Personal interaction and mentoring is the glue that holds an organization together.

When distributors hit those "rough spots" in their business, the coaching and advice that they receive from their sponsor...upline...downline...crossline... whoever ... is what keeps their steam going.

See what you're really getting paid to do is manage an organization. Help your people succeed. Develop leaders. Something that no automated system can do.

No automated system will ever be able to replace human leadership and the ability to manage a group of people. Every person is different and is going to need individual guidance and direction in their path to success. It takes a human being to do this.

And that is why you'll never get paid for doing nothing.

Plus, all systems – no matter how automated they are – still require a human being to monitor and manage them. There is no perpetual machine that runs completely on its own steam. There still has to be someone who puts gasoline in the tank...starts the engine...operates the gas and the break pedal...and turns the steering wheel.

However...despite the trap that one can fall into when relying on systems, they are truly an indispensable piece to a successful network marketing business. *It's just important to know w*hat they can and can't do for you.

5. WE HAVE THE BEST PRODUCT EVER!

Now it's not that this statement isn't necessarily true (although often it isn't)...it's that it doesn't matter.

This lie takes on many different forms. Here's just a few of the variations:

– The product sells itself!
– Nothing else on the market can even compare to this! We have the most lucrative comp plan in the industry! Our leadership team is unbeatable!

Each one of these assertions could go off on their own little tangents, but really what they all boil down to is this: Network marketers place all the emphasis on all the wrong things.

It's not that all these things (product, company plan, leadership, etc.) aren't important. These are all critical elements.

The problem is that while everyone is hootin' and hollerin' about this stuff, they forget about the most important factor of all.

To illustrate this problem, consider investment properties for a moment. There's an important lesson to be gleaned from real estate that can help shed some light on the situation.

It's often said that the three most important factors in choosing investment in real estate are: (1) location, (2) location, and (3) location.

If you're looking at a piece of property from an investment perspective, you shouldn't be admiring the beautiful perennials out back...or concerning yourself with how many kids the neighbour has...or noticing how well the drapes go with the carpet. If you are, you're looking at it through the eyes of a home owner, not an investor.

In order for your endeavour to turn out profitably, you have to keep the main thing the main thing.

Well just like real estate, when it comes to running a highly-profitable business, a similar formula needs to be applied. Namely the most important factor of all is: (1) Marketing, (2) Marketing, and (3) Marketing!

This may seem obvious to you, but think about how many people go running around, diving headfirst into one company after another, following the latest and greatest product, only to end up scratching their heads when they don't make any money.

Just as focusing on things like the landscape, the flowers and the neighbours is the way a home buyer looks at a property rather than an investor...putting all your focus on things like the product, the comp plan and the corporate leadership is the way a consumer looks at a company rather than a business owner.

6. YOU JUST DON'T HAVE ENOUGH BELIEF!

The evil lie of motivation and belief has got to be one of the greatest shams in the history of sales (not just network marketing).

Millions of distributors everywhere are told that the reason they aren't successful yet is because they just don't have enough belief. Or they don't have a big enough "why." Don't you just want to lose your lunch when some big shot in front of the room tells you that?

The heavy hitters in your company would have you believe that you just need to get to that "breaking point" where you're sick and tired of being sick and tired and then...nothing will be able to get in your way!

So what do you do? You listen to inspirational CDs. You cut out pictures of the car you want to buy and the places you want to go. You put those pictures everywhere – your fridge, your dashboard, your cupboard doors, your computer monitor – so you're constantly reminded of what you're working so hard for. You think positive. You go to every meeting you possibly can to energize your battery and "pump" yourself up for the week. You go to the annual national rally because you know that just seeing all those massively-successful stars up on stage will be enough to kick you into overdrive. You'll be so overwhelmed and inspired that you'll be unstoppable! You'll reach that magical turning point where everything starts working and your bank account is filled with cash!

7. THE PROVEN SYSTEM

The so-called "proven" business plan is a broken-down, rusted system that's composed of faulty techniques and out-dated methods. And the worst part about it is that not only doesn't it work, it's severely harmful to your business (and your social life).

The only thing that the proven system is proven to do, is cause massive failure.

According to the annual reports of many mlm companies, along with research done by numerous tax preparation services, only 1-2% of network marketers earn substantial incomes.

Similar studies indicate that 97% of network marketers never reach a positive cashflow in their business.

These sobering numbers give solid proof to the fact that the strategies and techniques being taught only work for a very small percentage of people.

Please understand, when we refer to "the proven system," we are not talking about network marketing itself, but the way people build network marketing.

The techniques being taught are So bad that they make this business as difficult as it possibly could be and success becomes nearly impossible. Distributors literally have all the odds stacked against them.

Let's just re-cap what we've already covered:

- Many times people are lied to about the fact that they're in sales.
- Distributors are either provided no sales training or the training that is provided is extremely poor and ineffective.
- Most of the sales methods commonly used are annoying "used car salesman" tactics that involve tricking – even lying – to your prospect, cramming information down their throat and relentlessly hounding them for the close.
- The idea that anyone can do this business leads to the "thrown-'em-up-against-the-wall-and-see-who-sticks" mentality that is largely responsible for the attrition rate in this industry.
- Because of the lack of good sales background, most people resort to hype and over exaggerated claims to win over customers and prospects.
- Way too much emphasis is placed on motivation and belief...while the real rock-solid fundamentals of sales and marketing are ignored.
- Distributors are given the impression that because their company's product is the greatest and their compensation plan the most lucrative, they're guaranteed success. This is far from the case.
- Distributors are told that *everyone* is their prospect...which leads to millions of network marketers pestering the living daylights out of every human being they cross paths with...creating enemies of this industry in their wake and all the while seeing no results for their efforts.

No one who knows anything about marketing would ever, in their wildest dreams, try to sell to people who have no interest whatsoever in their product – let alone people who are downright hostile to it! Yet that's exactly what network marketers are taught to do!

Sales can be challenging enough as it is, let alone trying to do it when you've got two strikes against you by using crummy techniques.

The whole model of coffee appointments, home parties and hotel meetings completely ignores the real key to success, which is this: getting the customer to come to you first.

People never want what's forced on them! And that is precisely the problem with everything we've ever been taught about recruiting. All those motivational speakers just tell you to waste more time, energy and sweat chasing people. And when it doesn't work – get this—you're supposed to do even more of it.

That's like telling a drowning man to drink more water!

Here's another lesson that the proven business plan fails to take into account: More important than the company...the person...the product...or even the message...is the market!

If you're not selling your opportunity to people who genuinely crave what you have, you're always going to be trying to force a square peg into a round hole!

You can be selling the tastiest burgers in the world but if no one's hungry, no one's going to buy.

There are millions of people who are actively trying to figure out how to make money from home. What good marketing does is stand right smack dap in the middle of this flow and catches people when they're hottest – while they're seeking solutions to their problems.

It enters the conversation that's already going on inside their head and gets them to take action.

In order for a business owner to be successful, they have to have a system that consistently does this for them over and over again. You hold up your end of the bargain and a good system will produce for you. It has to be fool-proof.

One of the most important functions of your system is that it needs to make sure you're only spending your valuable time with the highest quality people.

Prospecting simply means sifting and sorting through people to find the ones who are interested. The sheer volume of lead flow you need to have coming into your business is impossible to achieve if you try to do it all yourself on an individual basis.

Doing it the old manual-labour-make-a-names-lists-and-ask-for-referrals way is like using a typewriter to bang out 10,000 letters when you could have a printing press do it in a fraction of the time.

A finely-tuned marketing system should do this sifting and sorting for you automatically.

It's like a machine used in a manufacturing plant: You put raw materials in one end, it spits out qualified results—prospects—on the other end. Predictably and consistently, 'round the clock. Every day when you wake up you know it will produce new potential business partnerships for you to cultivate.

The problem that most network marketers face is that they spend so much time prospecting, they don't have time to actually sell.

Once you implement an effective marketing system, you can spend twice as much time in front of interested people and literally double your results immediately.

❖❖❖

9

STEPS TO EFFECTIVE NETWORK MARKETING

There are countless reasons why so many people start a network marketing business, and sign on worldwide. In an increasingly uncertain world, more of us are seeking an alternative to the traditional pattern of study, work, and retire. Those willing to sacrifice family, friends, and leisure pursuits to the demands of a corporate employer are decreasing in number. Men and women alike are realizing that the best security in life is self-reliance.

Although the dream of owning your own business is appealing, statistics paint a more realistic picture of long hours, high stress, and low returns for small- to medium-size business owners, who struggle to make a profit after deducting costs for leasing, inventory, staff, and operations.The answer is network marketing, an opportunity to own your own business without taking on the burden of going it alone. It's an entrepreneur's dream.

Here's how network marketing works: As an independent representative (also known as a distributor, associate, consultant, member, or business owner) you form a partnership with a corporation that provides a product or service along with administrative and marketing support.

With the corporation taking care of the back end of the business, you are free to focus on the frontline actions that produce income.

Your income comes from selling products or services, and from recruiting others to sell products or services. The higher your total sales, the higher your income.

What makes network marketing so attractive is that it costs almost nothing to start and very little to run. There is no up-front capital investment required, apart from a small outlay for a starter kit, so you can own your own business without using your own funds or having to borrow capital.

There is no ceiling on what you can earn, and you don't have to sacrifice family and friends to join the highest echelon of achievers.

Most network marketers run their business from home, and they work it around their everyday life. Some opt to supplement the household income by working their business part-time while they, their spouse, or both of them continue in traditional employment. For others, their network marketing business is the sole source of household income.

Couples pooling their skills and resources to build a net-work marketing business together are becoming more common, allowing family to take center stage in their lives.

No one way works better than others. The point of network marketing is to provide freedom and flexibility to fit your personal ambitions and circumstances. What counts is that you get to decide what's best for your life.

Network marketing is one of the few businesses where you can earn as you learn, right from the start. If you find yourself faltering:

— Think of the millions who labour through years of university or college for a chance to join the ranks of the higher-income earners.

— Think of the millions who invest their own capital in a business only to end up working horrendous hours trying to make it pay against all odds.

— Think of those who waste their life stuck in traffic, as they commute to the office and back.

— Think of those who miss pivotal events in their children's lives, due to work commitments.

— Think of those who dread going to work each day to boring, repetitive jobs, not to mention having to work with and for people they wouldn't spend time with under any other circumstances.

— Think how lucky you are that you are at the helm of your own low-risk, high-reward business—business where you get to decide how your time will be spent and with whom you will spend it.

Here are the three rules of network marketing:

1. *There are no shortcuts*. As with any endeavour, if you want to succeed you must be prepared to work hard, and work smart. And that starts with mastering the skills that have been proven to work by the millions who have already built successful businesses.

2. *There are no excuses*. If something isn't working for you, you have to be prepared to change. That doesn't mean looking around for a better company, a better system, or a new idea. It means changing *you*. Perhaps your attitude, the way you present yourself, the way you communicate, or your understanding of how the business works. This book will help you determine where to focus your

time, energy, and resources to enhance your chance of success.

3. *There are no trophies for trying*. Network marketing rewards results. Not everyone will make it because not every-one is prepared to do what it takes. If you *are* prepared, the rewards you receive will make it all worthwhile. If you decide network marketing is not for you, you will have risked nothing and lost nothing. One of the strengths of the industry is that you can even keep your regular job while you are buil:d-ing your business.

This chapter will give you specific information and guidance related to your products and your business opportunity. It will guide you step by step toward your most ambitious goals. If you are willing to learn and willing to work, you will create the life you and your family deserve and become a role model for others who dare to dream big dreams.

DARE TO DREAM

Imagine you have been granted three Wishes. What will you wish for?

> More excitement? More adventure? More freedom? More money? More time? More fun?

The only limit to what we can achieve in life is the limit of our imagination. Every achiever—from the scientist who achieves a medical breakthrough that saves millions of lives, to the sportsman who overcomes all odds to break a world record—started with a dream.

Imagine the first settlers to land on American soil know Misconceptioning next to nothing about what they would find here, but with hearts bursting with dreams for a better future.

Imagine the first person to gaze up into the night sky and dream of landing on the moon. At the time, it must have seemed beyond impossible. But it happened, because someone dared to dream.

Life is not about following a path that others set for us. It's about blazing new trails to create the life we choose.

Dreaming frees us from our doubts, our skepticism, our prejudices, our past experiences, and the expectations of others, to reveal the truth of what we want in life. Our capacity to achieve has no limit, if we dare to dream big dreams.

Take time to consider what will make you, and those you love, truly happy. Ask six simple questions:

1. What do I want to be?
2. What do I want to do?
3. What do I want to give?
4. What do I want to have?
5. How do I want to spend my time?
6. With whom do I want to spend my time?

When you know the answer to these questions, you gain awesome power over your future.

However long it takes for you to decide how you want to live your life, it will be time well spent, because when you know what matters most to you, you will move mountains to make it happen. Lackluster dreams never inspired great deeds or amazing feats.

Think how we respond to events that touch our hearts. Think how we rally behind our favourite causes. Think of the lengths you would go to protect your family and the people you love. The more passion you have, the more energy you will generate to make your dreams come true.

Too many people live in a drab world of black and white. Too many allow self-doubt and uncertainty to quash their dreams. Not you. Think vivid, vibrant colour.

This is not the time to hold back. Set your imagination free and let it soar.

SET YOUR SIGHTS

Now its Time to Turn Your Dreams into Goals

Dreaming kindles our imagination and ignites our passion, but goals are tangible destinations that we set before we set out on our journey. Knowing what you are working toward will focus your energies in the right direction and keep you on the right track.

The purpose of a goal is to take you from where you are to where you want to be. Therefore, goals have to be realistic. That doesn't mean forgetting your dreams, but rather setting progressive goals, or mileposts, that will take you toward them, one step at a time. Set your first goals no more than one year ahead. There will be time to focus on new goals once you achieve these first ones.

No matter how impatient you are to start work, know that one of the most common mistakes made by entrepreneurs and corporate business people alike is being impatient.

The time you spend identifying your priorities is never wasted. Having the discipline to clarify your goals is one of the keys to success.

Ask yourself, "Are my goals realistic in my current situation?" If you set your sights too high, you will quickly be come disillusioned. Success is a great motivator. It's better to set modest goals and achieve them than to overextend yourself and fail. As your circumstances change, so can your goals. As you achieve each goal, set your next one until, step by step, you find yourself stepping into your dream.

BELIEVE YOU CAN

Henry Ford is Quoted as Saying 'If you think you can, or think you can't, you are right." He was right.

Belief is the fuel that drives network marketers and you will be as strong or as weak as you believe yourself to be. You need:

- Belief in your business
- Belief in the company you choose to partner with
- Belief in the products you represent
- But most of all... belief in yourself!

When you believe in yourself, you free yourself from the expectations and actions of others and equip yourself to deal with the inevitable swings and round abouts of normal business growth.

Self-doubt will slow you down. If you unload your doubts before you get started you will be able to move faster and more smoothly toward your goals.

It's easy to say, "Believe in yourself," but many of us harbour feelings of doubt or inadequacy. So let's look at how you acquired your beliefs in the first place.

Beliefs were most likely formed when you were young— from messages sent to you by your parents and other influential people in your life, such as your peers and teachers.

Not all of us had the good fortune to grow up in a nurturing environment surrounded by people who knew the importance of building self-esteem. People who cared about us may have sent the wrong messages from inexperience, or because they were mirroring their own insecurities.

Whatever your past experiences, you can start cleaning your slate whenever you want. It may take time, but every step is ground that you have gained from your enemy—lack of belief in yourself and in your right to have, and be, the best.

You can start by accepting that belief comes from within, and taking responsibility for your feelings of strength or inadequacy. As an adult you are free to form your own beliefs. Your past is in the past. You are now in control of your life.

Ninety percent of all communication is self-talk. Playing negative tapes over and over inside your mind will only deepen the groove of negativity in your brain and stifle your ability to achieve your goals. You may as well play positive ones.

Start by listing all your great qualities—your warmth, your compassion, your vision, your honesty, your intelligence, or your creativity. Look for areas where you excel. Think of what a loving parent, partner, son or daughter, or friend you are. Think of the determination, focus, and energy that have brought you to this point in your life and all the good things you have done. Think of where you started and how far you have already travelled in life.

Filter criticism. If it's valid, thank the person who did you a favour (even if it doesn't feel like it at the time) and consider it a chance to grow. For example, let's say you've been told you are too lazy to build a successful network marketing business. But wait. The problem may not be laziness. Lazy people don't start their own businesses or set goals to change their lives. It may simply be that you are overwhelmed with responsibilities or carrying unresolved issues that sap your energy. In that case, take a step back, and decide what's important in your life, and what you need to let go.

You are not your blunders or slipups. The only people who get things right all the time are those who play it safe and never attempt anything new. Can you imagine anything worse? You deserve a more exciting, fulfilling life than that, even if that does mean risking a few spills.

Remind yourself that the judgement of others will be clouded by their own personalities and experiences. You are you: unique and wonderful! You can be whatever you want to be, have whatever you want to have, and live the life that you thought only dreams were made of when you believe in yourself.

If you are among people who make you feel insecure, start to loosen ties with them and seek out positive, enthusiastic, and supportive people instead.

Top up your self-esteem with every positive feedback and compliment you receive. By filtering out the bad and absorbing the good, you will become stronger emotionally.

Above all, learn to separate fact from fantasy. We have two sides to our brain: rational and emotional. Our *emotional* side is reactive and helps us respond swiftly to potential danger. When there is no real threat we sometimes allow our emotional side to create unnecessary stress.

Our *rational* side is proactive. We use it to make decisions and solve problems based on reason rather than emotion. We are using the rational side of our brain when we question the beliefs we hold about ourselves. Learn to differentiate between the two when you find yourself under pressure. Try to put a distance between the issue and the resolution. Time is a great clarifier.

Make a conscious decision to be as kind to yourself as you are to others. Don't waste time wallowing in past mistakes, and focus instead on the person you will become. Just because you couldn't do something before, doesn't mean you can't do it now. Tell yourself, "That was then, this is now." You can't drive forward if your eyes are fixed on the rear-view mirror.

If you have genuine personal issues to deal with, don't despair.

Nobody is perfect. Focus on your strengths, and allow yourself to grow as you build your business and your life.

Identify weaknesses and start working on them. Negative thinking without a specific plan for improvement is self-destructive and pointless. That's why we call it *stinking thinking!*

You will need to be strong, because it is the nature of network marketing that we continually have to put ourselves on the line. Rejection goes with the territory. You can't avoid rebuffs or mistakes, but by believing in yourself you will be able to weather good times and bad.

Building a healthy self-esteem is not just about you. Your confidence will filter down through your organization as it grows. By working on your self-belief you are not only helping yourself, you are developing skills that will enable you to help others. The more strength you have within, the more you will have to give and the more likely you are to build an organization of loyal, committed people.

WORK THE PLAN

When you are clear about what you are Working for you are ready to focus on how you are going to get it. It's time to take a look at how different companies pay their representatives.

Every network marketing company has a compensation plan (sometimes called a marketing plan) that sets out clearly what you have to do to get what you want.

The common denominator of all legitimate plans is that payments are based on the sales you generate, both from personal sales and the sales of people you recruit. The higher your total sales, the more you will earn. If you are lucky, the plan will be simple and easy to understand. But many plans seem confusing and complicated, especially to newcomers. Compounding the problem is that many are bogged down by insider-speak, or jargon.

Don't be deterred. As the business has developed, so have the plans. Most good ones specifically focus on key behaviours required to build a successful downline organization. A strong *downline*—that is, the people you recruit and train and from whose sales you also earn a commission—is at the heart of success. As you learn the plan, you are learning what you must do to maximize your income.

If you understand the plan you can explain it clearly and enthusiastically to prospective recruits. When you do a good job they, in turn, will be able to explain it clearly and enthusiastically to their prospective recruits. Now your entire organization is focusing on the most productive areas.

This is what you need to know regardless of what plan you are working with:

> The most basic principle of network marketing is duplication—selling product, and recruiting others to sell product and recruit others, over and over and over. This is what all plans are designed to encourage and reward.

You will be paid a percentage of the total sales you generate, usually monthly, although some companies work on four-week, two-week, or one-week cycles.

Your percentage will increase as you reach and maintain higher levels (also known as ranks). This is designed to encourage you to build your business and reward you for consistent performance.

Your rank is based on your personal sales and the sales of everyone you recruit, both directly (known as first levels) and indirectly (the people your first levels recruit down the line, known as second and third levels, etc.). Collectively, these people are known as your personal group (or downline).

When a member of your group recruits enough people and produces enough sales to achieve a higher rank, they are known as a *breakaway*. You are paid on your breakaways, but at a lower rate, as the leader of that group is expected to support her or his own people, freeing you to find and develop more recruits.

Those who develop the most breakaways reach the highest ranks of most plans—and consequently the highest rewards. A few superachievers receive monthly payments of hundreds of thousands of rupees or more. But they earned their rank the way you must, by recruiting one person at a time. How quickly you reach each rank will depend on how hard you work and how skilled you are at marketing your products and your business opportunity.

If you grow your business steadily, your income will rise month by month, subject to the fluctuating demand for your products throughout the year.

Most companies allocate approximately the same percentage of total sales to pay their representatives. However, each company structures its plan slightly differently. As one example, some plans pay a small percentage on the sales of everyone you recruit, whereas others require that you recruit a set number of people and reach a combined sales target before you are paid on your recruits. Another example is the difference in how much you have to sell personally to earn higher commissions.

DON'T REINVENT THE WHEEL

When you Signed the independent representative agreement to start your own business, you probably heard, "You are in business for yourself, but not by yourself." That pretty much sums up what network marketing is about.

Although you are 100 per cent responsible for your results, you selected a corporation to be your business partner. Whatever your reason—you fell in love with the product, you liked the plan, or someone offered you a great opportunity—you are now in a powerful partnership.

Unlike the majority of self-employed who struggle to build their business with borrowed capital and high overheads, you now have a partner with enormous resources all at your disposal. You are effectively running a small business with all the resources of a large one. Maximize your advantage by making the most of all that is available to you. You pay only for the resources you need, so there is no waste.

Your future and that of your corporate partner are linked. The more successful you are, the more successful the corporation will be. The corporation wants you to succeed.

It's important that both sides establish and maintain a good relationship based on mutual understanding, trust, respect, and loyalty.

Each corporation is unique, with its own culture, products, plan, track record, and role models—all of which are living proof that the system works. From day one, you have access to this reservoir of resources. Seize that advantage.

You may not like everything your corporate partner does. Remember that the corporation is in partnership with a wide range of representatives, each with different goals and circumstances. It is unrealistic to expect everything to fit your specific needs.

As with any business, mistakes may be made from time to time. These are not deliberate (chances are you will make a few too). Have faith in your choice of company. Slipups are frustrating but they are not the end of the world unless you choose to make them so.

For example, a popular product that suddenly goes on back order is an inconvenience, but it is also an opportunity to trumpet the soaring demand for the product to your customers and recommend they keep an extra one handy, or order sooner during promotions (when popular products are promoted, sales often exceed company forecasts).

Cultivate a good relationship with the person who recruited you (your upline) and the people farther up the line who recruited that person. They all have a wealth of knowledge and experience to share with you through training and mentoring. They want you to succeed—the more successful you are, the more successful they will be. By learning to accept differences and avoid judgments you will foster great relationships with a myriad of personalities.

Above all, don't try to reinvent the wheel. Adopt your corporate partner's system. It has worked for others before you. Learn it, follow it, and duplicate it by example and through training.

Don't waste time creating your own resources. You have talented staff to do that for you in your corporate office— free!

The more time you spend at the frontline of your business, marketing your products and your business opportunity person-to-person, face-to-face, by phone, and by e-mail, the faster you will rise through the ranks. Time spent on activities that do not lead to recruiting, booking appointments, or selling product is time wasted.

TAKE CHARGE

However, good your company, your products, or your plan, your success is up to you—100 per cent.

The only person who can guarantee you will achieve your goals is the person who owns them—you. From Day One, you are founder, president, and CEO of your own business.

There may be no "I" in team, but there is in win. Nor is there any limit to what you can achieve when you seize control.

By taking responsibility, you're not vulnerable to the performance of others, and you're free to focus on what you need to do to achieve your goals.

When things go well, this will be easy. But what about when things don't go according to plan? Do you have the strength and courage to accept responsibility through good times and bad?

Life is not perfect, and it is unrealistic to believe that everything will go your way all the time. You will get your share of good luck, just as you will get your share of bad.

It's easy to look to the company, your upline, your group, or just bad luck when your business stumbles or falters. But the moment you do so, you relinquish control. When problems arise or your strategy isn't going according to plan, you have an opportunity to become stronger and develop new skills—skills that you can pass on to your recruits when they strike trouble.

Have the courage to make bold decisions, take action, review the consequences of your actions, and make more decisions. Decide, act, review; decide, act, review;...

When you accept that "If it's to be, it's up to me," you gain awesome power over your future.

WORK THE HOURS

The system works if you do. At first you do more than you get paid for, but then you get paid for more than you do. That's what residual income means. It's income that keeps coming after you have done the work. But first you have to do the groundwork.

Think of an oil field. You know there's oil out there somewhere, but nothing is going to happen until you drill holes. Some will be dry, some will strike oil, and some will tap rich veins. The more holes you drill, the better your chances of striking oil. Once you have tapped a rich vein, the oil keeps pumping as long as you maintain the pumps.

It's the same in this business. There are no easy answers, magic formulas, or insider secrets to reveal. The number of hours you invest working your business will determine what you achieve and how quickly you achieve it.

This business is simple, but it's not easy. That's why the rewards are high for those who succeed. Commit action time to your business and the results will follow.

Practice makes a man perfect. When you're working, note what works and what doesn't, make the necessary adjustments, and keep working. Small improvements every day add up to significant improvements over time.

You can be different. Work every day without exception, and work as many hours as you can. Industry research clearly shows that people who work their business consistently have significantly higher incomes than those who work erratic hours. Make daily lists, and work steadily through them. Work the phone, work the Internet, work the room, and work your community. The more people you connect with, the greater your chance of success. Take your business seriously. Allocate specific times to work, and refuse to allow anything or anyone to intrude on that time. Just because you don't have to clock in doesn't mean you can take it easy. Cheat on your hours and you only cheat yourself. If you feel yourself flagging, take a closer look at the goals you sprinkled around the house to remind yourself what you are working for.

We all have different body clocks, but mornings are when most of us are fresh. Start each day with a *Power Hour* working the key aspect of your business—making calls! You'll feel energized for the rest of the day, knowing you have dealt with your most important task.Whatever happens, don't put off doing what you must do to achieve your goals. Activity leads to results, and results lead to rewards. Procrastination is a fast pass to failure. When we delay important tasks, we don't forget them. We carry them around with us and, as the day draws on, the burden becomes heavier. Even a small load will start to feel heavy after an hour or two. By tackling the tough jobs first, you will feel lighter for the rest of the day.

MASTER SIX CORE SKILLS

One of the benefits of network marketing is simplicity. Master three core skills and you are well on your way to success. Master three more and there's no ceiling on what you can achieve.

Imagine a toolbox. Inside, there are six tools to help you build a network marketing business: three basic tools for the simple tasks and three for the slightly more complex ones. The sooner you master each tool, the sooner you will get results.

Let's start with the basics.

1. *Scheduling.* Your planner is the only indicator of your business. A planner full of bookings and appointments means your business is in good shape.
2. *Selling.* Your monthly check will depend on how much product you, and the people you recruit, sell.
3. *Recruiting.* Your business opportunity is your flagship product, and you won't succeed until you learn to promote it effectively.

Now we come to three advanced tools that will help you realize your most ambitious goals:

4. *Building Relationships.* One-off sales and chance encounters will not build a strong business. If you are constantly working to find new customers and prospects, you will burn out before your business is secure.
5. *Mentoring.* Your success will ultimately depend on the success of the people you recruit. Although you are not responsible for their success, you are responsible for the quality of support you give them.
6. *Managing.* Chaos does not make for a successful business. As your business grows, you will be juggling more than a few balls. You want to drop as few as possible.

There are only six tools, and you must master all of them. If you don't learn to schedule, it won't matter how good a salesperson you are, because you will have no appointments. If you don't sell product and the people you recruit do not sell product, your check will hardly be worth cashing. You can't be a mentor without people in your downline. Businesses don't run themselves.

No one will expect you to be perfect at the beginning. Don't be afraid to tell people that you are learning. They will appreciate your candour, and they may be encouraged to follow your lead when they see you don't have to know it all to get started.

SELL, DON'T TELL

No one gets paid until product moves. Your personal sales generate income as you build your business, and they set an example for your recruits to follow. The higher the total sales of your group, the higher your monthly check will be.

Start by becoming your own best customer. First, you will have no credibility if you expect others to buy your products when you are not buying them. It's your personal story that people will respond to, not a long list of features and benefits.

Building a loyal base of customers who use your products will guarantee you a steady income. Look for lifetime customers, not a quick sale, and you will be on your way to creating residual income.

If you belong to one of the growing number of companies that ship for you, or that offer an auto-ship programme, take advantage of it. But stay in touch. If you lose contact you lose future sales and you lose a potential recruit.

Any sales transaction with integrity should involve four actions:

1. *Start a relationship with your customer.* The stronger the ties you build with your customer, the more likely it is that you will make the sale, and many more for years to come. Don't fall into the "one-size-fits-all" trap. Each customer is unique, with different needs, interests, and ambitions that will help you identify the products from which he or she will benefit most.
2. *Show your customers how your product will make their life better.* In this age of instant gratification most of us are looking for products that offer simple solutions—to help us look a little younger or a little more attractive, to feel better or have more energy, to lose weight, to save money, to reduce stress, or to cancel out our bad habits. Don't complicate matters by telling your customers more than they need to know to buy. Find out what their issues are and show them how your product will make them right.
3. *Close the sale.* When you close, move confidently. Reassure hesitators with your belief in the product.
4. *Follow up to ensure that you have a satisfied customer.* Never lose sight of the fact that you are looking for lifetime customers. Make sure you make your customers feel good, whatever decision they make. Always promise that you will be calling to see how they enjoy their product, and/or keep them informed about upcoming promotions. It is much easier to say, "I promised to call to check how you are enjoying your products," than to have to explain why you are calling. If you don't make the sale say, "I'll stay in touch, if that's okay with you." When you have permission to call, you are more likely to make the call, and make it confidently.

RADIATE POSITIVE ENERGY

To build a quality business you need quality people. The best way to attract quality people is to become a live advertisement for your business.

We are attracted to people who have the qualities we wish we had, so the image you project will determine how others respond to you. First impressions are especially important when you are constantly reaching out to new people. Each time you walk out your door, you create a positive or negative impression.

We all want to be successful. But if the price is too high, people will turn away. When you project stress, pressure, and tension, potential recruits will think, "Thanks, but no thanks."

Slow down, allow for the unexpected, and give people your full attention. When you find yourself rushing, take a deep breath.

You are not only marketing an income opportunity. You are marketing quality of life. To do so you have to embody the qualities of someone enjoying quality of life. Financial success without balance is a hollow victory.

Not everything will go your way all the time. Learn to love the business for all that it brings and accept good times and bad as two sides of the same coin. Whatever challenges you are experiencing, project an aura of confidence, happiness, and calm. Your charisma will soon attract the people who will help you build a dynamic business.

FOCUS ON RELATIONSHIPS

Your company may be amazing, with a to-die-for compensation plan, brilliant incentives, and staff who will go to the ends of the earth to serve you, but there are other companies out there with great plans, incentives, and staff.

Your training programmes and support systems may be state-of-the-art. But with the fast-moving advances in technology, anyone can mimic those advances as fast as they are developed. The only thing that cannot be copied, or imitated, is the relationship you build with others.

It takes five times the effort and energy to find a new customer or replace someone in your downline than to keep the one you have. So it will come as no surprise that the top tier of achievers spend most of their time developing relationships with their downline, whereas their less-successful counterparts are forever working to replace people who are leaving.

Relationships need both quantity and quality of contact to develop.

Start with your customers. It takes discipline to follow up all sales with a "satisfaction" call, and to service your customers regularly. But in the long run, you will save time because you will not be forever chasing new business, and you'll increase your chances of a customer becoming a recruit.

The wider you spread your net, the better your chances of finding customers and recruits. Nurture relationships with neighbours, colleagues, suppliers, and others within your community. The more people you know, the better your chances of finding potential recruits, and sparing yourself the painstaking process of cold calling or scattering flyers about town.

We like people who like us, and show genuine interest in us. Put your ego aside and give the people you meet your complete attention. Maintain eye contact, and don't allow yourself to be distracted. Learn to ask questions and listen to and remember the answers, so when you next meet you will have meaningful conversations instead of superficial small chat.

If all this does not come naturally, work at it. Look for common threads—family, friends, interests, work, and local issues. Bonds will build faster and stronger when you find interests or beliefs in common.

As you build your organization, your ability to build relationships with the people who paid you the compliment of joining you will be a key factor in your success. Never be so busy finding new people that you neglect those already in your group.

As your downline grows, you will find yourself working with a mix of personalities. Recognize that everyone has different goals, styles, and viewpoints. Great businesses are built on a diversity of skills and experiences.

You will generate loyalty by offering the best training and support you can, based on each person's circumstances and needs. Small gestures—such as promptly returning calls, remembering special occasions, and acknowledging milestones—can make a big difference. Turning off your cell phone when you are with others shows you respect their time.

Your new recruits need close contact as they transition from reliance to independence. The bond you build with new people may stop them from walking away before they have given their business a fair chance of succeeding.

Focusing on new people and those who make the biggest contribution is sound business sense, but it takes little effort to make everyone feel valued. People stay where they feel important and appreciated.

As your business grows, you will have increasing pressures on your time. Set an example by building strong relationships with your first levels. Your example will encourage them to build strong relationships with the people they recruit right down the line.

You want everyone to feel the pride that comes with belonging to an organization with a genuine commitment to helping people achieve their personal goals.

KEEP IT SIMPLE

The path to failure is paved with detail. I've lost count of how many times I've watched from the sidelines as customers lost interest during a sales presentation or prospects switched off halfway through a lecture on the company's compensation plan.

Make "keeping it simple" a driving philosophy throughout your business. Start with the way you market your products and business opportunity.

Words will not convince people to buy your product or get excited about your business. The fewer words you use, the more time you will have to spend on what really counts—getting to know prospects, finding out what they want, and showing them how you can make it happen.

The average commercial on television is thirty seconds. Why? Because that's what works! Any shorter and the advertiser will struggle to make the point; any longer and the viewer will start flicking channels. How do advertisers create commercials that hit home in such a short time frame? The same way you will create commercials for your business. By focusing on simplicity and impact.

Decide what you want to say and edit your words to bring out the magic. It's not what you leave in, but what you leave out that counts, unless you want to be talking to minds that are closed to incoming traffic.

When you overexplain your products, you insult your customers' intelligence. If they want to know more they will ask, and they will listen more intently because it interests them. Party planners will find that sales and bookings flow from parties that are lively, informative, and interactive. Too much information will guarantee a stodgy, uninspiring event.

Keep your business presentations short, ideally no more than forty minutes. Spend the first third getting to know your prospect, the next third sharing the key points of your business based on what you learned. Spend the last third answering questions and deciding on the next move: signing the agreement, scheduling another meeting with a spouse, giving your prospect literature to read and agreeing to follow up the next day, or passing.

Assume that everyone is busy. Always let your prospects know how long the appointment will take. Never exceed that time. People will relax when you respect their space and schedule. Full-time workers will be more willing to meet with you if they know they can meet for a chat over a sandwich and return to work within a one-hour lunch break. You can always schedule a second meeting.

Apply the same discipline to opportunity nights or business seminars. Plan to take no more than ninety minutes from start to finish. Greet guests as they arrive and let them know you appreciate the time they have taken to learn about the business. Let your starter kit, recruiting literature, and key products work for you by displaying them where guests can look, read, and touch.

Keep the formal part short and stimulating, leaving time for interaction. Overrun your time and your guests will stampede toward the exit the first chance they get. Finish talking while they are still intrigued... and you'll get your chance to close the deal.

Although it takes work and discipline to make things simple, your efforts will pay dividends when you get results.

BECOME AN EFFECTIVE COMMUNICATOR

There are few born communicators. Most of us have to work at developing our communication skills.

The best communicators understand that people are incredibly self-centred. Need convincing that this is true? Picture what happens when you are shown a photo taken with family or friends. You immediately scan the photo for yourself! No matter how lofty our dreams to be selfless are, self-centeredness is a fact of human nature.

It follows that people will respond to you when you talk about them. Your prospects will come from different backgrounds and will have different experiences and perceptions. They will filter everything you say through the beliefs and prejudices they have formed throughout their lives. You can't expect your message to hit home if you are taking random shots..

When you speak less, you have to make every word matter. Black and white tells; colour sells. Colour your conversations and presentations with stories and anecdotes. Bring your products and business opportunity to life with personal experiences and compelling examples.

Avoid industry jargon, especially when you are prospecting or interviewing. Use everyday language with your customers, prospects, and raw recruits can relate to. If you are talking about new concepts, check with your listeners by asking, "Does this make sense?" or "Am I explaining this well enough?"

A significant portion of communication is visual. When we like what we see we are predisposed to like the message. Before you even open your mouth, your audience is deciding how credible you are and how interested they are in what you have to say.

The quality of your voice also makes a strong impression. Your timbre, pace, and volume will convey confidence and credibility or insecurity and insincerity. Voice quality can be learned, and it will pay dividends if you fix problems you may have. It's okay to be nervous but there's no excuse for being flat.

Our eyes are the mirrors to our thoughts. Maintaining eye contact not only flatters your audience, because you are talking directly with her, but it enables you to tell when your listener's interest is waning. When you see it happening, change your pace, tell a story, or ask a question to win back her attention. There is often a fine line between a "Yes" and a "No" decision. Ignore your prospect's perspective, override her concerns, or let her mind wander and you diminish your chances of hearing that magnificent question, "How soon can I start?"

Communication is a fundamental skill in any people business. You will not reach your peak without becoming an effective communicator. If you lack confidence, have difficulty with technical aspects of communication, or want to fine-tune your presentations, get outside help. Many excellent courses on public speaking are available, and organizations such as Toastmasters can help you become a better communicator.

KEEP FINDING NEW PEOPLE

The only way to grow your business is to consistently introduce fresh faces. The day you stop introducing new people is the day your business will start sliding backward.

New people will add to your sales volume and, if you inspire them, introduce more new people. They will bring new ideas, excitement, energy, and momentum, and they will be living proof to everyone in your group that people want to join the business.

A strong business needs both width (people you personally recruit) and depth (people recruited by the people you recruit). There is no better way to get your people recruiting than to introduce a parade of new people yourself.

In an ideal world, rely on people would be wonderful if these things worked. But when you rely on others you abdicate responsibility for the success of your business to them. This makes no sense.

The First Rule of Recruiting

The first rule of recruting is numbers. If you recruit only a small number of people you will be at the mercy of their individual performances. The more people you have in your group, especially first levels, the more invincible you will be.

The Second Rule of Recruiting

The second rule of recruiting is *balance*. Balance comes from having enough personal recruits to insure you against the stellar performance of one person (leg) of your business. Don't rely on one or two "stars" to produce your volume. Discovering a stellar performer in your downline can be an intoxicating experience.

Depend on one person to produce a disproportionate share of your results, and your business becomes vulnerable to the performance of that person.

Besides, the more breakaways you develop, the faster you will rise through the ranks to the top levels where the highest incomes are earned. Your chances of finding potential breakaways rises with every new person you recruit.

The Third Rule of Recruiting

The third rule of recruiting is to look for people with the desire and the drive to move up the ranks quickly. Think about where you are most likely to see stars.

Outstanding leaders know the best way to build their businesses is to surround themselves with the best people they can find. Network marketing is no different. Set your sights on potential leaders. Start with people who are already successful at what they do. Look for bright sparks who have yet to reach their potential. When you look up, you will see stars.

Broadening Your Reach

Prospect for recruits in the places that best fit your organization. Think: *Who would be interested in the business, why would they be interested, and how will I approach them?*

If your system is business oriented, plug into business and professional associations. Wellness centers, medical suites, fitness centers, and spas are a great fit for health products. If you are a party planner, fill your planner with demonstrations, classes, spas, and parties.

It's always easier to find people like ourselves. But the wider range of people you recruit the better. Look for people who bring fresh skills, attitudes, and experiences into the team, not just those you find easy to approach. The secret to a winning team is balance.

Never assume any prospect will not be interested. Hundreds of thousands of people from all walks of life join this industry every year to achieve financial freedom without risking capital, and without sacrificing family, friends, and leisure time. There is only one guaranteed way to lose a recruit, and that is not to ask.

Although your strategy should be to build your business with quality people, don't prejudge. Everyone deserves a chance. If it doesn't work out, the person will have risked nothing and lost nothing, except the opportunity to make money; work from home; learn new skills; become more confident; and have more time for leisure, traveling, and making new friends.

BECOME A MENTOR

There are few nore rewarding roles in life than to be a mentor, and the catalyst for another person's success.

People will enter your business with a wide range of abilities and goals. The majority will always work this business on a casual basis. The collective sales of these small producers can produce significant volume.

A few are destined to become top performers. These perfect candidates for mentoring will identify themselves by their results. They are your future breakaways—leaders with the potential to inspire, motivate, train, and support their own people. The more breakaways you develop the greater your chance of long-term success.

Being a mentor takes energy and commitment. For the relationship to work, the commitment must be mutual. Focus your attention on performers who earn your support by what they do, not what they say. Don't be dazzled by someone who talks the talk until they show that they can also walk the talk.

Being new to the business should not stop you from becoming a mentor. Think of the relationship you have with your children. You don't profess to have all the answers but you care about them, and you know their strengths and what they can achieve. You share your knowledge and values with them, give them your full support, and allow them space to grow—mistakes and all.

If you run your business as you raise your kids, you will become a powerful mentor. Sharing your vision and experience, establishing expectations and guidelines based on the goals your stars set for themselves, and offering honest feedback and support along the way will empower them to reach their fullest potential.

Think about how you teach your kids to play board games. You teach them the rules and then take turns to move. When they make a wrong move, you suggest alternatives ones, until they become skilled players: Your move, my move, your move, my move...

Approach mentoring the same way. Your goal is for your recruits to become confident leaders who will, in turn, pass on their skills and experience to the people they recruit. If you do too much for them, or make too many allowances for non-performance (remember that they set the goalposts), you are doing them no favours. Think, "Your move, my move, your move, my move..."

Mentoring can be time-consuming and it can be tempting to let your personal sales and recruiting activity slide while you focus on your prote´g´e. But balancing your time between personal activity and coaching others makes business sense. Although you have taken on new responsibilities, if you stop doing the things that brought you to this point, you will stop growing. Besides, when the person you have mentored becomes the independent leader you knew she could be, it's time to mentor someone new. You won't find that person unless you maintain a flow of people into your business.

EMBRACE THE TOOLS

Do you have to incorporate new technologies into your network marketing business?

Only if you want to succeed!

Most network marketing companies invest heavily in sophisticated technologies for their representatives. It makes sense to take advantage of them.

Technology gives you a competitive edge over "traditional" businesses, which have become increasingly weighed down by administrative costs, government regulations, and unproductive staff. It allows you to run your business efficiently, and concentrate on the frontline activities that create your income.

Let's start with the most basic of all: a sales transaction. The Internet has transformed the way we shop. For every person who shops online, there are hundreds more who research products online before they buy.

The Internet makes it possible to send information to many people quickly and cheaply. It allows you to personalize bulk messages and to produce a regular schedule of fresh messages and follow-ups—everything you would do if only you "had more time."

When you send an e-mail newsletter out to your customers you can see who opened it. Calling them is much easier when you can say, "Did you see anything you liked in this month's specials?" Party planners can see who clicked on the link to party or host invitations. Your well-timed follow-up sales call could turn a "maybe I will/maybe I won't" into a party guest or host.

And what about keeping yourself abreast of news? New telephone technologies make participating in a telephone conference call or seminar an efficient way to learn new techniques, receive upcoming promotions and products, and hear company news first-hand.

Many companies offer teleconferencing, teleseminars (by phone), or Web conferencing (on your computer) at no cost to you, but even if you pay to participate, there are still enormous savings in time and travel costs compared to attending a meeting or conference.

Technology makes managing your business easier. When you have an Internet link to your corporate partner you can track results and spot instantly where to invest your time and energy. By monitoring your business on a weekly or even daily basis, you can provide instant recognition to those who are progressing and give tangible support to those who are struggling. It's like having an office in the corporate building—only better!

Behind the front line, there are many consumer-friendly computer programmes to help you deal with your business and tax obligations efficiently, freeing you to concentrate on the activities that create your income.

High-tech tools, and the terms that describe them, may initially overwhelm you. A bewildering array of buzzwords has evolved to describe these new tools. Don't let words intimidate you. The engineers of these tools know that they have to be simple to use, or they won't sell. They are designed to make life easier for you.

The bottom line is that the Internet is your ultimate tool. It is your link to your corporation, your customers, your downline, and your upline. It enables you to develop a global business from your home office or kitchen table.

Developing an Internet strategy for your business will put you on an equal footing with your competitors.

Keep your website fresh and topical. It is your shop window and will work well for you if it is updated regularly with new products, tips, or information to keep customers interested.

If managing your own website is not your strong suit, look for ways your corporate partner can assist. If your corporation does not yet offer that support, you'll find help in the Yellow Pages. Or, you may need to look no further than your own family.

A word of caution. For all its advantages, the Internet can't perform miracles. Like any tool, it is designed to help you, not do the job for you. It has to be used in the right way, at the right time, and in the right place. It is not a substitute for personal contact. Nevertheless, taking advantage of all the tools that have been created to help you look after your customers and maintain your business will free you to concentrate on the person-to-person interaction that is the magic of network marketing.

KEEP MOVING, WHATEVER HAPPENS

Momentum is everything. You cannot fail in network marketing if you keep moving. It's fine to set your own pace, based on your personal goals, abilities, and circumstances. This is not a race. There will always be people who progress faster and slower than you. Staying the distance to achieve your goals is what counts, however long it takes. The hare and the tortoise both crossed the finish line.

Sometimes you will progress faster than others. Other times you'll encounter unexpected roadblocks and have to backtrack, or take a detour or two. But if you set out with the certain knowledge of where you want to go, and the determination to do whatever it takes to get there, the only way you can fail is if you stop moving.

A mature business attitude is critical to success. You will set yourself up to fail if you believe that things will always go your way, or if you feel discouraged when you progress at a slower pace than you planned. Every single step you take is a step toward your goals. Expect your journey to be challenging and you won't be disappointed when you encounter difficulties. You will find a way to keep moving, whatever happens.

Starting out is the easiest part of network marketing. The strength to keep moving when the going gets rough is the true test. Too many people in this industry give up after the first few bumps. Not you. Accept that the journey will have adrenaline-rushing dips and peaks. Every challenge you overcome will make you stronger and better equipped for the next one.

If you are serious about success, you cannot afford to let outside influences affect you. You have to believe:

— cannot control what happens to me, but I *can* control whether I allow it to affect me.

— cannot control what other people say, do, or think, but I *can* control my own thoughts, words, and actions.

BEND, DON'T BREAK

Achievers in any field know how important it is to be flexible. A mountaineer expects that the climb will not be a straightforward ascent. He anticipates having to find a way around obstacles, or backtrack to find a safer path as he climbs to the peak. Any successful CEO understands the unpredictability of the markets and knows she must respond quickly and confidently when the need arises.

It's the same for you. You are not building your business in a vacuum, but in the real world, where you cannot control your environment.

When everything is firing, it's easy to feel unstoppable. Perhaps you are on target to move up a level in the compensation plan, earn a car, or achieve a trip to an international seminar.

Then, just when you thought nothing could go wrong, everything does. Someone you counted on lets you down. A promised sale doesn't come about. A hot prospect changes her mind at the eleventh hour.

It's natural to feel frustrated when your best-laid plans are thwarted. But the sooner you accept that it has happened, the sooner you can start doing whatever it takes to get back on track.

Birds constantly correct their path in flight. Changing weather conditions, the appearance of predators or prey, and the flight path of other birds may all call for a change of direction, position, or speed. And pilots, despite the most advanced navigation technologies, keep making adjustments to hold the airplane to its flight path.

It's the same in business. You have to keep correcting, correcting, and correcting to stay on course.

Nowhere will flexibility matter more than in your dealings with customers, prospects, and downline. Like all people businesses, network marketing can be volatile. Your people will have different aspirations. They will think and learn differently and respond to different stimuli. Where one person sees black, another will see white. Expecting everyone to think and act the same will inhibit your chances of success, as will trying to persuade others to understand your point of view instead of seeking to understand theirs.

Being flexible is critical to survival. The more quickly we adapt to our ever-changing environment, the more we improve our odds of success.

If your strategy is not working, ask, "What am I doing, or not doing, right?"

When Plan A isn't working, you have to switch to Plan B. If Plan B comes unstuck, develop Plan C. You won't solve a problem by continuing with the strategy that created it.

MANAGE YOUR PRIORITIES

There will always be twenty-four hours in each day—no more, no less. Yet busy people make the best recruits, and busy people fill the top tier of this industry.

Somehow, they find time to do what they want to do. Their secret? Understanding that they can't control time, but they can control how they use it. It's all about setting priorities.

When you plan your day, ask yourself three key questions:

1. "Will this help me make more bookings or appointments?"
2. "Will this help me recruit more people?"
3. "Will this help me make more sales?"

Although your goals may take years to accomplish, your activities should focus on the present: "What needs to be done now?"

If you spend your day rushing from task to task, chances are you have yet to learn to choose what's important and what's not. Time won't expand just because you have lots to do. You have to take time *from* one activity to give *to* another.

Successful people forgo small indulgences every day to bring their dreams to fruition. Learn to say "No" unless you are willing to sacrifice your dreams to someone else's agenda. There is no honor in being a martyr.

The hardest door to get through will always be your own. By practising self-restraint, and by applying big doses of discipline to your day, you will be able to enjoy unforgettable experiences: company-recruited trips to exotic locations, money to spend on luxuries like no-expense-spared family vacations (and the time to enjoy them), a mortgage-free home, the best education for your children, the means to support your favourite charity, your dream car, or—the best of all—never having to worry about money again.

If you are feeling overwhelmed, you may be attempting to be a superhero. Accept that you are not. Asking for help is not a sign of weakness. Trying to be all things to all people is. When you ask someone for help, you are paying that person a compliment.

There are few surprises in this industry. The winners win because they deserve to. They know the path to success is travelled one step at a time, one day at a time. They concentrate on taking small steps each day to bring them closer to the future they dream about. They know what is important, when to ask for help, when to delegate, and when to say "No."

Decide what's important to you and put it at the top of your To-Do list each day. Don't waste time on minutiae that eats up time better spent achieving your goals, and don't spend your day darting from task to task.

Plan each day the night before so you can start working on productive activities first thing the next morning. Here's the best way to write an effective To-Do list:

1. Make a list of everything you want to do.
2. Do a reality check. Can you get everything done or do you need to move some items to another day?
3. If your list is overloaded, what needs to go?
4. Look for ways you can make your day smoother. Save time by writing the phone numbers next to the names you must call. Look for ways to combine two trips.
5. Rewrite the list with the most important tasks at the top.

Next morning, start early. If unexpected circumstances arise, you will already have gone through a good portion of your list.

FIX WHAT'S FAULTY

There are only two reasons why people fail in this business: not working hard enough or not doing it right. The most common fault is that they do not work hard enough. Success is 10 percent inspiration, 90 percent perspiration. If you are not working enough hours, it is unrealistic for you to expect to reach your target.

If you are working hard but still not seeing results, then you are not doing the right things. You may have the best intentions, but if it isn't working for you, it's time to find the fault and fix it.

Every move you make is working for you or against you. There is no neutral ground—your business will move for-ward or backward based on the actions you take.

Each of us has unique strengths that we can draw on, and each of us has our limitations. It makes sense to work from your strengths, and it makes just as much sense to eliminate the weaknesses that will hold you back.

Start by pinpointing where the problem is. If you are not meeting enough people, focus right there. If you have the leads but are struggling to find takers, do some serious work on your approach. If people join but don't perform, take a look at who you are recruiting, how you are training, and what support you are giving them. You will not move forward until you fix the weak links.

Never blame others for your lack of progress. Focus on yourself and what you can do. When you own the problem you own the solution. The key difference between people who make it to their destination and those who end up on the sidelines is the willingness to take responsibility.

No one gets a free ride. You may get one or two lucky breaks, but they won't exempt you from having to learn and apply the skills necessary to succeed.

Sometimes your technique may simply need fine-tuning, but be prepared to make major changes if necessary. If you have a flat voice, no matter how excited you are on the inside, people will not respond. Invest in voice coaching. If you don't know as much as you should about your products, use them more often and dig out the product manual. If there are aspects of your business you haven't yet grasped, make an effort to learn them. Knowledge bolsters confidence and credibility.

Be prepared to ask yourself tough questions: "Does my enthusiasm come across as pushy or desperate?" "Am I really a good listener or am I just waiting for a pause in the conversation so I can have my say?" You won't get far if you are broadcasting when you should be tuning in.

Can't pinpoint the problem? Swallow your pride and ask for honest feedback from people whose opinion you respect.

The stakes are too high for you to let your missteps determine your future, or to waste your chance at success by stopping when you reach the limit of your current knowledge, experience, or ability. Have the courage to rise beyond your previous performance peak, and you will reap the rewards.

LEAD GENERATION

Lead generating methods are always a debate in the circles of distributors in the network marketing business. Some believe in generating their own leads, while some think that buying leads is quite easy to build their business very high. New distributors or beginners in this network marketing business often don't have a choice and wonder who is right in generating leads for the business. The fact is both sides of the distributors are right on their own experiences and success. Most of the distributors have got massive success that means they have started earning six-figure income or more.

The two lead generating methods have their own ups and downs. Generating own leads help in capturing quality leads, perhaps the quantity of leads would be very less when compared with the other method, but the distributors can gain more trusted and honest leads for their business. This is very important for the long-run and success of the business.

Most of the personally generated leads always respond to the distributors query. While, leads purchased online tends to reject the distributors query and never share requested information. It takes large of time in generating own leads and it is really difficult for the beginners in the business. Most people spend hours on generating leads, but it is worth for the long-time success in the business. With buying leads, marketers need not have to worry much about generating leads because they will get enough leads according to their payment.

In generating own leads, distributors are free to follow and use their own methods. Also, this method is very helpful in branding themselves and also the products, and most importantly distributors can gain wide recognition among leads. Also, marketers can capitalize themselves for the profit of their business. Purchased leads are applicable to only certain methods and also the leads are sold to multiple distributors. Therefore, this reduces the chances of increases the profit in the business.

Each lead generating methods have different pros and cons. The marketers can choose any method that works best for them and also the one in which they feel highly comfortable.

GET TRAFFIC TO YOUR NETWORK MARKETING SITE

When you are in the network marketing business, in order to make money, you will need to have customers. In order to have customers, you must have a good domain name and web hosting programme that will draw traffic to your site. In order to make sure that you have the right domain name, you can check with Google's Keyword Tool. The tool will allow you to see keywords that are searched on a monthly basis. When you are selecting keywords, choose keywords that are at least two words long. Make sure that the keywords that you choose have at least 4,000 monthly searches.

Go to the domain site that you want to purchase your domain name from. The next step is to type in the keywords that you have chosen. Make sure that you are able to get a .net or .com. If they are taken, try to find some other keywords in the Google Keyword Tool that will allow you have a .com or .net site. More people search the Internet using .com. Go to a web hosting site. You can find the best web hosting site by searching for the top 10 best web hosting sites.

Some web hosting sites offer domain names. If you want to have more than one domain, this may be an option for you. If you are unsure on how to get set up, the web hosting company will get you set up for free. The company should have a number that you can call them, just in case you ever need them. Once you are set up, you should expect to get more traffic to your site. If you have a product that customers want, they will more than likely purchase it.

You could start to double your income by having the right domain name and web hosting site. You will start to wonder why you didn't do this a long time ago. In order to have a successful business, you must have the right tools. All successful business owners were able to get traffic to their site by using the right tools.

DO NETWORK MARKETING ALONG WITH YOUR STUDY

Many college students have hard time getting the extra money that they need to pay for books and personal expenses. There parents may not be able to send them money, so they have to locate a part-time job while attending school. Many businesses do not like to hire college students since they prefer to hire full-time staff. A college student can earn some money while attending school by getting into network marketing. The student should have a personal laptop computer, so that they can work anytime of the day or night.

Locate a network marketing company by visiting a home business forum that offers a network marketing folder. Search the folder for a list of network marketing companies that you can join. If links are provided, click on each link to see what the network marketing company is all about. Before choosing a network marketing company to join, ask other members in the forum about the company. The other members may have done business with the network marketing company and can provide any positive or negative feedback.

Join the network marketing company of your choice and create a free blog. Post banners and pictures of the products on your blog. Write product reviews on different products to let potential customers know how a product is before they make a purchase. Some network marketing companies will send you samples of their products. It will be helpful to try out the product before writing a review since you can provide an honest review about the product.

Promote your blog on social networking sites that you visit. Read the sites policy on self-promoting before posting your blog. Whenever you make a comment on a friend's page, just post a link underneath your comment. Their friends will see the link and may become curious and click on the link. Place a short description underneath the link to let potential customers know about the product that you are selling. It should include the benefits and any specials that may be going on.

While you are in class, you may be able to gain sales. You do not need to be on your laptop all of the time to make a sale. Since your blog will reach a large audience, anyone can make a purchase. You may even be able to get customers from your class.

❖❖❖

SELECTED READINGS

Achrol, R. S. and P. Kotler (1999), "Marketing in the network economy," *Journal of Marketing*, 63, 146-63.

Allen, Douglas E (2002), "Toward a theory of consumer choice as sociohistorically shaped practical experience: The fits-like-a-glove (FLAG) framework," *Journal of Consumer Research*, 28 (4), 515-33.

Barábasi, Alberto-László(2003), *Linked: The New Science of Networks*, Perseu Book Group [Journal of Marketing Research Book Review] [*Journal of Marketing Research Book Review*].

Bornholdt, Stefan and Heinz Georg Schuster (2002), *Handbook of Graphs and Networks: From the Genome to the Internet*, Wiley-VCH.

Dahlstrom, R. and R. Ingram (2003), "Social networks and the adverse selection problem in agency relationships," *Journal of Business Research*, 56 (9), 767-75.

Ellis, P. (2000), "Social ties and foreign market entry," *Journal of International Business Studies*, 31 (3), 443-69.

Ellis, Paul and Anthony Pecotich (2001), "Social factors influencing export initiation in small and medium-sized enterprises," *Journal of Marketing Research*, 38 (1), 119-31.

Ford, David Ed. (2002), *Understanding Business Marketing and Purchasing*. London: Thomson Learning.

Henderson, Geraldine R. (2004), "Consumer Associative Networks as Process-Tracing Measures of Brand Feedback Effects," in *Handbook of Marketing*, Manfred Bruhn (ed.), Gabler Press.

Hopkins, Nigel, Geraldine Henderson and Dawn Iacobucci (1995), "Actor Equivalence in Networks: The Business Ties That Bind," *Journal of Business-to-Business Marketing*, 2, 3-31.

Ozcan, Kerimcan (2001), "Modeling Word-of-Mouth and Consumer Choice in the Network Society," in University of Michigan Business School Working Paper. Ann Arbor, MI.

O'Donnell, Jayne (2011). "Multilevel marketing or 'pyramid?' Sales people find it hard to earn much". *USAToday*. Gannett Company.

Reingen, Peter H. and J. B. Kernan (1986), "Analysis of Referral Networks in Marketing - Methods and Illustration," *Journal of Marketing Research*, 23 (4), 370-78.

Reingen, Peter H., Brian L. Foster, Jacqueline Johnson Brown, and Stephen B. Seidman (1984), "Brand Congruence in Interpersonal Relations: A Social Network Analysis," *Journal of Consumer Research*, 11 (3), 771-84.

Rindfleisch, A. and C. Moorman (2001), "The acquisition and utilization of information in new product alliances: A strength-of-ties perspective," *Journal of Marketing*, 65 (2), 1-18.

Swaminathan, Vanitha and Christine Moorman (2003), "Marketing Networks and Firm Performance," Working Paper, University of Pittsburgh.

Swaminathan, Vanitha and Christine Moorman (2003), "Success in Network Markets: The Role of Network Size, Timing and Resources," Working Paper, University of Pittsburgh.

Wathne, K. H. and J. B. Heide (2004), "Relationship governance in a supply chain network," *Journal of Marketing*, 68 (1), 73-89.

Watts, Duncan J. Watts (2003), *Laws of the Web: Patterns in the Ecology of Information*, Massachusetts Institute of Technology Press [*Journal of Marketing Research Book Review*].

Webster, C.M. and P. D. Morrison (2004), "Network Analysis in Marketing," *Australasian Marketing Journal*, 12 (2), 8-18.

Wuyts, S., S. Dutta, and S. Stremersch (2004), "Portfolios of interfirm agreements in technology-intensive markets: Consequences for innovation and profitability," *Journal of Marketing*, 68 (2), 88-100.

Wuyts, S., S. Stremersch, C. Van Den Bulte, and P. H. Franses (2004), "Vertical marketing systems for complex products: A triadic perspective," *Journal of Marketing Research*, 41 (4), 479-87.

Zig Ziglar; John P Hayes, PhD (2001). *Network Marketing for Dummies*. Hungry Minds.